CW00663004

International Education Leadership:
Stories From Across the Globe

Catarina Song Chen

Lindsay Prendergast

Dr. Wallace Ting

SchoolRubric

Copyright © 2022 SchoolRubric Inc.

All rights reserved.

ISBN-13: 978-1-7378643-1-8

DEDICATION

This book is dedicated to all those who have served as international education leaders and to those who dream of doing so. Without the wisdom, insights, and experiences of the thirteen leaders inside this book, who carry decades of experience across countless countries, we could not have provided this important resource for the global education community.

We also dedicate this book to the educators working in our international schools for their tireless ethic, relentless optimism, and belief in global citizenship. And to our international school students: we also dedicate this book to you, those who bring a unique and valuable dynamic into our communities, and who we believe will one day change this world for the better.

ACKNOWLEDGEMENTS

SchoolRubric Publishing and the authors of this book would like to thank the following individuals and organizations for supporting the publication of this book:

Dr. Robert Thornell
Dr. Ann Marie Luce
Richard Siegel
Rebecca Findlay
Terri Lee Paulsen

READ WHAT OTHERS ARE SAYING

"What better way to learn about being an international school leader than learning from the best? I thoroughly recommend this collection of great stories from great practitioners, helping us build our own practice so we can give our kids and our own communities a much better experience."

- Kevin Bartlett
Founding Director, Common Ground Collaborative

"I believe that the brave stories of these authors will illuminate our current individual experiences and help expand our collective identity as leaders in international school communities. Like me, I hope that you drink from their stories and quench your thirst for connection, understanding, and identity, so that we can be ready for what is next!"

- Madeleine Heide
Retired educator and international school director

"The wisdom you'll find in this book from my global colleagues will feel resonant and meaningful for anyone working in an international educational context because the struggles - and victories - remind us we are not alone in our commitment to build a better world."

- Dr. Kristy Dempsey
Children's Author
Manager, Marketing Content and Creative Development
The Lumistella Company

"As leaders we are rarely doing or dealing with something completely new or unique that has not been done before so we can learn so much from the collective experiences of others, particularly their triumphs and their learnings. This collection of writings allows us all to learn from those experiences and build the approaches and strategies to meet our own challenges."

- Andy Paige-Smith
CEO, Academy of International School Heads (AISH)

"Reach for this book, international educators! Leaders and teachers should avail themselves of the practical detailed coaching, rich experience and inspiring possibilities offered by a remarkably gifted and experienced array of colleagues."

- Dr. Heidi Hayes-Jacobs
Founder & President, Curriculum Designers
International education consultant, Author, Futurist

"The reflections and learnings from the seasoned and thoughtful practitioners shared in this book are a huge gift to all of us striving to make a meaningful and enduring difference to the kids in our charge. The authors share from genuine, daily experience in the international school context, and draw on the growing knowledge base on leading and learning."

- Bambi Betts
Director, The Principal's Training Center

"I found it exhilarating and fascinating to hear the story that these great leaders from all over the world have shared and learn what I can bring back to schools and colleagues that I work with. I encourage anyone in education leadership to read this book!"

- Dr. Robert Thornell
Chief Executive Director of Learning and Teaching, Lewisville ISD

"We learn so much from veteran leaders like those that we find in this volume, and this collection of stories that they put together on topics including management of a school, how to improve a school, the roots of curriculum and instruction, attracting high-quality faculty and staff, and also looking at equity and cultural responsiveness is an essential read for any leader."

- Dr. Katie McKnight
Founder, Engaging Learners; Career educator

"The people in this book are true leaders, and legends, in our world. This book will give you the overview needed to understand why we all sincerely love this international education community and the world that we're part of."

- Laura Light
Executive Director, AAIE

"Who needs 180 days when you can go around the world in 13 chapters! Navigating the complexity, challenge and promise of international education can be difficult, but thankfully this intriguing compilation provides a compass."

- Myron Dueck
Educator and Author, *Grading Smarter Not Harder and Giving Students A Say*

"The book captures the essential commitments that school leaders must make: to unearthing the 'Why' of our values, to building community, to leading with integrity, to using effective tools (whether for communicating, planning, assessing or transforming), to be authentic as people and learners...and to be intentional about all we do."

- John Roberts
Certified Executive and Team Coach
Former international school director
Doors Wide Open Coaching Systems www.dwopen.com

Stories From Across the Globe

Table of Contents

Stories From Across the Globe

Table of Contents

1

Introduction

Lindsay Prendergast & Dr. Wallace Ting

International schools represent almost 13,000 institutions across the globe as of 2022 (ISC Research, 2022). They span a myriad of forms and frameworks across hundreds of countries all over the world, and yet we are united by a common purpose: connecting cultures, people, and nations through education. Leading today's international schools, no matter the location, presents unique challenges and opportunities made ever more exciting by the enticing adventures of living amidst a community of multinational, multilingual backgrounds. There is no single "education system" and yet schools are guided by standards for teaching and learning that reflect a vision of global schooling no matter the geographic location. As such, international school leaders of every type - Heads of School, Director, Superintendent, Principal, and others - must develop sophisticated leadership practices that enable nimble stewardship of diverse communities amidst cultural contexts which may or may not reflect their own backgrounds. International education is itself a community of such practitioners who, despite being located hundreds or even thousands of miles apart from another, are deeply interconnected and offer a powerful network of support and mentorship to new and aspiring leaders in this realm. This book endeavors to gather some of these voices in one single space for the future - and current – educational leaders to examine, and enjoy, the lessons of their careers.

The authors of these chapters are either current or former international school leaders, scattered across 11 countries. Their leadership lessons, and stories which illustrate them, are framed under standards of leadership delineated by several of the world's leading international education organizations: Association for the Advancement of International Education (AAIE), Academy for International School Heads (AISH), The Principal's Training Center (PTC), as well as accrediting organizations such as Cognia and even renowned education leadership frameworks such as Kouzes & Posner (YEAR). They are augmented by the work of such school leadership values and improvement frameworks as The Common Ground Collaborative. Such standards support schools in aligning their daily work to develop impactful systems that ensure the highest levels of student learning, and each of these chapters illuminates a personal experience of an individual leader navigating the complexities of upholding this purpose. As these leaders have woven their greatest lessons from decades of guiding schools in communities of every size and setting, a mosaic of experiences presents the underlying theme: international education brings the world together.

As a new or aspiring international school leader, the expanse between what has been studied in theory and what can only be learned in practice is vast. Learning from experienced leaders such as Lee Fertig (The Nueva School, United States) as he articulates the nuanced components of an effective teacher supervision program, or from Dr. Ruth Allen (The Columbus School, Colombia) and her deep background in organizational management, could typically only be accomplished in a conference setting, or a fortuitous personal encounter; however, the chapters of this book reveal not only the entertaining adventures of some of the world's most experienced international school directors, but they convey practical leadership lessons from actual schools and real scenarios. Imagine having a coffee conversation with Dr. Audrey Menard (International School of Panama, Panama), Dr. Bill Johnston (retired leader with 30+ years in international education), Dr. Colin Brown (American School in Taichung, Taiwan) and the entire cadre of leaders here in one afternoon, and you get a picture of the richness of this book.

Dr. Jeremy Moore (American International School of Johannesburg, South Africa) and Dr. Mary Ashun (Ghana International School, Ghana) bring us into the complex journey of building a cohesive and purposeful mission and vision; Bridget McNamer (Sidecar Counsel) inspires us to believe in the capacity of international schools to lead the field in ensuring equity across our entire school community; Robert Rinaldo (GEMS American Academy Abu Dhabi) and Dr. Michael Johnston (Frankfurt International School) examines how we can ensure learning is authentic and purposeful across our school. Dan Yamasaki (Colegio Panamericano, Colombia) reveals lessons learned for post-pandemic success within professional context from an international context, and we learn from Dr. Spencer Fowler (The Affiliated High School of Peking University's Dalton Academy) and Lisa Perskie (School of the Nations) about facing the challenges of tomorrow with new approaches to student-centered education.

Each of these leaders, through their diverse backgrounds and rich experiences, offers a powerful lesson gained from years in the field and captured here to catalyze the connection for rising leaders between what they know today and where they aspire to become the future generation.

It is abundantly clear from the massive growth of international education - nearly doubling in student enrollment in ten years (ISC Research, 2022) - that the world is demanding a new form of education, one that will match the sophisticated needs of a global society. As such, schools will require innovative, progressive leaders who are adept at guiding communities to deliver their mission and vision with nimble skills. While few institutions exist to explicitly prepare educators for the unique experiences of international education, the stories and lessons within this book seek to fill a need where the authors herein can share authentic examples that connect to explicit leadership values and practices. We hope you enjoy!

Data - ISC Research. (2022, February 24). ISC Research; iscresearch.com. https://iscresearch.com/data/

2

Forward

Catarina Song Chen

Educational reformer John Dewey believed that "Education is not preparation for life; education is life itself." If education is indeed life, school leaders are tasked with an enormous responsibility to ensure that students become lifelong learners.

To be a lifelong learner means having the necessary skills and mindset to grow continuously. The goal is not just adapting to survive, but also evolving to thrive. To remain relevant in life requires skills to learn, unlearn, and learn anew. But these skills are not attainable without first having an open mind willing to listen to others, respecting different perspectives, and having the courage and compassion to take action.

As the head of school, we are the highest-ranking administrator charged with the most responsibilities for the successful, overall operations and management of the organization. How well we manage the school can be measured by the progress of everything from student academics, faculty performance, culture and morale, school enrollment, financial health, campus management and expansion, fundraising, to even board relationships. As heads of international schools, we are charged with the same responsibilities, but in the context of multiculturalism. This often involves transient stakeholders living in a geographical setting that is different from their place of birth or passport, multiple curricula, as well as different customs, culture, and languages. The international context adds layers of complexity to the already comprehensive school environment.

Having served as the head of an international school in Brazil for the past decade and a half, I have had the chance to lead our constituents through major overhauls. One major transformation includes turning around a fast-sinking school with less than 100 students and on the verge of losing its accreditation to a thriving school with 500 students with a growing waitlist and master plan for expansion. This accomplishment was achieved by monitoring volatile economic conditions with fluctuating currency, managing community safety through widespread diseases, monitoring risks and lawsuits, and marketing for school growth all while the school door was revolving with transient stakeholders and musical chairs were rotating with eight different board presidents. Without a doubt, I have gained invaluable experiences in governance, managing risks and crisis, legalizing school operations, obtaining licensure and accreditations, restructuring school programs, establishing partnerships with external institutions, safeguarding school budgets, marketing to targeted audiences, engaging stakeholders, building culture and morale, creating hybrid and co-teaching programs, developing fundraising programs, designing master plans for sustainability, and managing construction for school growth - just to name a few to the ongoing list!

These multifaceted experiences have refined my adeptness to identify patterns in communities, embrace conflicts (because they will occur even if you try to hide from it!), and to trust my intuition. My experiences have also made me realize how lonely it can be at the top and how I could have benefited with more support; and this is when I realized that there are not enough accessible or adequate resources and professional support in the area of international education management and leadership. That's where this book comes in.

Even with over 100 years of international education, we still currently lack meaningful and rich resources and professional development that genuinely prepare aspiring international school heads for the arduous job or that could provide continuous assistance for those that are already on the job and looking for ongoing support. Looking back to my first year as a head of an international school, I can't help but wonder, if given a chance to tell my younger self what I know now, what would I say? What are some pieces of cautionary advice or words of wisdom that I could share with my younger self, who first found the landscape of international schools intimidating, lonely, and nebulous?

I first became the head of Escola Americana de Belo Horizonte (EABH) back in 2009. I was a pioneer in my own right as the first and youngest Asian female to be appointed head of an international school in Latin America. Over time, I have become an anomaly as one of the few longest serving heads of international schools. I can now humbly admit that I have gained not only serviceable skills, but also extraordinary experiences and immeasurable insight by facing many challenges head-on and hands-on.

There was no textbook that prepared me in college; and there is still no current manual I can reference to guide me through the complex and sticky situations that international heads of schools often navigate, such as the interesting intricacies involved when working in another country and engaging with people of different customs, cultures, and languages.

This is why this book has been written. My wish is that this book will help fill a lacuna that currently exists in leadership of international schools. This book is created with the intention to serve as a guide. It's a handbook of authentic cases to prepare our leaders with realistic expectations as we forewarn of complicated challenges that may arise but also inspire creative solutions. These scenarios can be used as simulations when preparing for the future or can be examined as lessons learned to be applied in new situations.

International Education Leadership: Stories From Across the Globe is a collaborative effort to share stories that matter and are relevant to educators aspiring to become heads of international schools or anyone already involved in educational leadership. The excerpts are biographical accounts contributed by my amazing colleagues - renowned authorities who are well-respected in educational leadership for having made an impact in international education. This book offers a rare inside look of real-life accounts revealing vulnerabilities, hidden treasures, and reflections for the future.

Additionally, this collection of testimonies can also serve as qualitative data for researchers. It can be treated as case studies that offer in-depth examination of current situations in the international education realm. Research in this field is still scarce because of its niche market status despite its century long existence. But this is now changing very quickly.

The international school market is growing exponentially and, consequently, the need for high caliber heads of schools is increasing while recruitment becomes competitive. However, there is a glaring and ever-growing gap between the augmenting number of international schools and decreasing availability of qualified, responsive leaders. Another reason this gap persists is the lack of holistic and comprehensive training programs that prepare educators for international school headships. This book aims to connect the dots by helping to bridge the demand for international school leadership with confident education leaders, well prepared and ready to take on the role as heads of international schools. We hope to make these connections by equipping leaders with the necessary knowledge that can be acquired with our real-life stories which address the subtle, but powerful nuances of educational leadership that aren't commonly taught in master's courses or identified in professional standards.

Thirteen international education leaders have come together from across the globe to share lessons learned. The moral of international school leadership is captured in the book and divided into seven major motifs:

- Mission, Vision, and Core Values
- Professional Capacity of Educators
- Curriculum, Instruction, and Assessment
- School Improvement
- Community of Care and Support for Students
- Equity and Cultural Responsiveness
- Operations and Resource Management

Together, they illustrate the beautiful landscape of international school leadership; they turn an abstract work of art that paints everything tenuous, gray, and ambiguous in educational leadership into a clear form of tangible perspectives. The book unveils the mysterious skills of educational leadership to portray intuitive knowledge and perceptive accounts of lessons learned.

An aspiring head of school can learn firsthand with their own personal experiences or learn vicariously through the experiences of others. If you have the fortune of learning through firsthand experiences, then you can further your learning with the lessons shared in this book. If you have not yet been exposed to international school leadership, then this book will serve as an imaginative-reality playbook, your go-to guide filled with carefully curated stories to inform on what to expect when leading international school ventures and how to be response-ready with strategies that have been tried and tested.

Stories from Across the Globe serves to advance education with authentic and relevant accounts by action researchers who have already navigated the complex and multi-dimensional aspects of international school life, have tested, and tried pragmatic approaches and outside-the-box strategies, and most importantly, have decided to share their lessons learned with humbling reflections. May this book be the first of many more publications. May we learn together, forgive one another, and may our stories live forever.

"Anyone can hold the helm when the sea is calm."

- Publilius Syrus

3

The Compass of Leadership

Mission, Vision, and Core Values

Dr. Jeremy Moore

So, there I was, stuck in the middle of the North Sound, floating in the dark. The motor on my boat had sputtered loudly earlier in the afternoon, but it kept turning and moving me forward; I remember thinking that there was simply some water in my fuel line, so it didn't concern me, and I kept on cruising. But several hours later, night had fallen, and I was beginning to head toward home when I heard a loud crack from the manifold. It smelled of smoke and oil. The engine was hauntingly silent, and I was left completely without power. A few weeks earlier, I had purchased a new GPS navigating device and I had started doing some boating at night, using my GPS to confidently guide me from my home to fun restaurants and places that dotted the coast at various points of the island. That afternoon, the GPS was flashing, and on the way to the restaurant that evening it pulsed a final flash before it turned into a frozen screen that looked like the Space Invaders video game. As fate would have it, right after I lost my engine, I looked at my phone and there were zero "bars"—no service. The twinkling lights from the distant shorelines melted into the stars above. Without a working engine, GPS, compass, or phone, I didn't know where to go, and didn't know how to get there.

Being lost is not only physical; it can describe an individual's mental or psychological state and can also relate to organizational culture. As it is with many teachers, my first year as an educator was extremely challenging. Fresh out of graduate school, I was full of idealism, passion, and energy, thinking that I was ready to open the eyes of young children and instill in them a fire for learning, develop their essential skills, and inspire them to be the world's future change agents. The first class of my educational career was a group of 36 fourth-grade students, many of whom were loosely identified as "special needs," from an average public school in rural Georgia (USA). There was no learning support teacher, or aide or partner, and I had almost no educational resources. I was thrown into the deep end with no support or life line. My two "teammates" on the grade level were waiting to retire and were unhelpful, perhaps even subversive, and the school structures and curriculum were as clear as mud. The administration was focused on straight lines and quiet mouths, the culture was siloed and uncollaborative, and there was no identity or collective purpose that was evident or inspiring. There was no GPS or compass. What exactly was I to teach? What direction was I to take? I didn't know where to go, and I didn't know how to get there.

The success of any school is dependent upon the level of clarity and commitment to its purpose, the extent to which its beliefs are understood and upheld, the development of a shared vision, an effective roadmap for progress, and the capacity of its leaders and members to foster a culture that embodies its ideals. At some point in our lives, we have all felt rudderless and lost. In the absence of purpose and direction there is often a sense of loneliness, and by-products of being adrift can include apathy, ineffectiveness, and unhappiness. A school can lose its way too, but when its mission, vision, and values are deeply understood and lived, there is a North Star to follow. Then educators and staff are motivated and positive, students learn at higher levels, and the school community thrives. There is nothing more important for a school leader than the continual cultivation of the organization's purpose, principles, parameters, and path for its future.

Why are we here? The answer to this question is an expression of the heart and soul of a school and an articulation of its mission and purpose. A statement of purpose provides the foundation for a school's focus and direction, offers clarity, and creates connectedness and shared aspiration. When people come together in concert toward a common goal that is greater than themselves, there is a heightened sense of energy, creativity, collaboration, pride, and ownership in the work they do together. Studies show that organizations with a collective purpose, shared vision, and common values outperform those who do not (Senge, 2006). A school mission statement, or statement of its purpose, is not simply words thrown together for a single event and then left to be forgotten; it is the galvanizing representation of its reason for being.

There is significant power in expressing and codifying an organizational (or individual) purpose, and no one has emphasized this better than the author, Simon Sinek. In his seminal book, *Start With Why*, Sinek (2011) shares that every organization on the planet knows what they do (*whats* are easy to identify), some organizations and people know how they do what they do (articulating the things that make them different or better), but very few people or organizations can clearly articulate why they do what they do. In schools, we are oozing with altruism and inherent goodness; we are fortunate that we do not have to look far to find our why, but most schools and educational leaders do not engage in key conversations that focus on this core idea. Serving as the director at the American International School of Johannesburg (AISJ), I started a new school year by having the members of the leadership team write their own personal why statement, and I asked them later to connect this to the purpose of the school. We began the year by talking about why we were all there rather than what we were going to do. I led faculty leaders in the same dialogue, and at an opening session I asked everyone in the school to think about their personal connection to our collective purpose. No matter our role (bus driver, secretary, coach, gardener, teacher, etc.), all were encouraged to be an active part of our collective purpose as we engaged with children and with each other every day.

What do we believe, and what do we value? Fundamental "community principles" or core values that a school community embrace are cultural lighthouses and crucial guardrails for the behaviors of every member of an organization. In addition, "learning principles" articulate a school's central beliefs and understandings regarding basic tenets of teaching and learning. At Cayman International School (CIS), our educational teams collaborated with colleagues at the Common Ground Collaborative (commongroundcollaborative.org) to develop learning principles that were grounded in our fundamental philosophies of education. We merged our re-accreditation activities with our strategic planning events and streamlined the process of resetting our organizational direction. Ultimately, we articulated our beliefs about what constituted high-quality educational practices, set a more progressive tone for the school, and brought people together to launch into inquiry-based projects and interdisciplinary learning. At AISJ, our school community shared in a process called Voices to Vision. I engaged in numerous listening sessions (small and large groups, individual interviews, zoom meetings, etc.) that culminated with a large stakeholder event, facilitated by the Notosh group (notosh.com). Listening to students, faculty, staff, and parents, Notosh analyzed over 5,000 lines of data, 526 survey responses, 149 digital boards of information, 43 listening sessions, along with digital and physical sticky notes to begin a draft of our community beliefs. In our weekend stakeholder session, we collectively refined the drafts and, ultimately, we cocreated a set of community principles that reflected the cultural ethos to which we aspire. These guiding statements were a catalyst for a culture shift in the school community; established a new, more inclusive ethos; and formalized expectations for how we were to treat one another. Incorporating guiding principles that represented our intrinsic values defined how we behaved and acted as a community—or what any visitor would experience walking in our door. To design and build truly effective schools for the future, we need to think about, talk about, and ultimately come together to create educational and community principles we want to work and fight for.

Who are we? A concrete understanding of the identity of an organization is furthered and made increasingly transparent by an articulation of its parameters. Most schools share some basic characteristics and universal commonalities, but each and every school is unique and special in some way. In conjunction with core principles, some schools highlight parameters or delineate quantitative thresholds that help to define and explain their identity. Examples from international schools include declaring the primary language of instruction, limiting percentages of student nationalities or other demographics, specifying capacity of student support services, determining proportions of local and overseas staffing, focusing financial commitments to professional learning, identified programs or highlighted priorities, and a host of other defining indicators. Parents often choose schools based on values that align with their own, and a school's guiding statements help fulfill those expectations. Guiding statements and parameters can also help limit unreasonable parental demands that go beyond the school's focus. And perhaps the most important parameter of all is for schools to always base decision-making on student needs and the continuous improvement of the teaching and learning program. When precedents or transformative decisions need to be made, a school's parameters and commitment to its identity can provide essential guidance.

Where are we going, and how are we going to get there? The path that a school intentionally follows is a blueprint that brings action to a vision and a strategic plan. A vision statement is a picture of what an organization aspires to become in the future and an illustration of its intended direction (Senge, 2006). "The future is not a result of choices among alternative paths offered by the present, but a plan that is created—created first in the mind, and next in activity. The future is not some place we are going to, but a place we are creating. The paths are not to be found, but made, and the activity of making them changes both the maker and the destination" (Schaar, 1981, p. 257). By identifying ambitious goals that everyone shares, a school can build a framework and a plan for better teaching and learning.

An effective vision has the power to inspire us when it is cocreated and shared. If any one idea about leadership has inspired organizations for thousands of years, it is the capacity to hold a shared image of the future we seek to create. Such a vision has the power to be uplifting and to encourage experimentation and innovation. Connecting and relating with others around shared vision will ensure all rally around something that deeply matters. This collective energy builds trust, creates unity, promotes collaboration, increases communication, and brings clarity around what needs to get done (Senge, 2006). The right vision creates a community with shared meaning. As educators and leaders, we derive meaning by helping to create something bigger and greater than ourselves, using our creativity to build programs that help realize the vision and fulfill our professional and creative aspirations. We are inspired to see our work as more than just a job but rather a cause that lends purpose to our lives (Olverson, 2015). The practice of shared vision involves the skills of unearthing shared "pictures of the future" that foster genuine commitment and enrollment rather than compliance. When there is an authentic vision (as opposed to the all-too-familiar "vision statement"), people excel and learn—not because they are told to but because they want to.

A strategic plan is an indispensable tool that can help turn vision into reality. The process of developing a strategic plan needs to consider all school stakeholder interests, and the involvement of school community members can contribute to its overall success. In fact, it is essentially teachers who do the practical work of implementing action plans. Strategic plans are mechanisms of guidance, which means they must be clear and accessible, and useful for decision-making. Great schools are able to maintain focus on the most important things. A good strategy forces a school to be clear about what it wants to achieve as well as outline specifically how it will proceed. Schools must be ready and willing to adapt and revise their strategies and related action plans, as needed to always be effective in real time.

So what? Who cares? Statements of vision, purpose, and core beliefs should not be dismissed as empty words on a wall; but despite their significance and benefits, they are subject to a number of criticisms. They can be full of shallow marketing language that sounds good but has little impact on continuous improvement of teaching and learning. Staff members might not be aware of, or care about, what the guiding statements say. Even if they are posted in every room in the school, it is common for educators, students, and parents (and even leaders) to not know or understand the guiding statements of the organization, and this may mean the explicit values and intentions are disconnected from what actually happens in the school. Words can become dated, expressing values of generations past rather than the current needs and sentiments of the community. This is a common reality and a significant challenge in international schools that have transient populations and regularly experience high percentages of teacher and family turnover. Statements can also be vague and unrealistic, providing little guidance for putting the words into practice. And strategic plans that are supposed to outline and guide the vision into reality can be rigid or prescriptive, detailing multiple years of future action too precisely, rendering them ineffective in responding to current realities.

In my first year as head of Cayman International School, my

predecessor and the board had determined it was time to develop a new strategic plan because the date on the previous one had lapsed. I engaged with a consultant, brought together a large committee, and, over the course of a weekend, we went through the traditional motions of writing new statements and a strategic plan. After that process, the statements drifted into insignificance. Despite my concerted efforts to follow the scripted plan, many things changed at the school. The plan was no longer appropriate or valid, and it sat, gathering dust on a shelf. This was a pivotal learning experience for me in my career. As a leader, I had not ensured that the mission and vision were living statements of purpose, and I had not galvanized others in using the words and plans to inspire meaningful action. Three years later I had another chance, and the experience was extremely positive and transformative for the school. Ultimately, the process brought our entire staff together and focused deeply on a shared understanding of what learning is and how we make it happen. The level of clarity and synergy was greatly enhanced; we established a common language, broke down silos, and reached a new level of collaboration. The new strategic plan was inherently connected to our vision and provided guidance. We were inspired and we elevated our craft. We knew where we were going, and we knew how we were going to get there.

What do good leaders do? Whether individuals or organizations, we follow those who lead, not because we have to but because we want to; we follow those who lead, not for them, but for ourselves and a greater purpose - those who lead inspire us. One of the fundamental responsibilities of a school leader is to bring the organization's mission and vision to life. But this takes time to emerge; it is a perpetual process, and not even the most capable leader can accomplish it alone. The whole school must come together in a culture of collaboration and create synergy to reinforce the principles that guide everyone toward a preferred future. Feelings are more influential than thoughts (Kotter, 2008). Great leaders get people emotionally involved in the work and its purpose. Consider that "culture eats strategy for breakfast" (Drucker, 1959, p. 28). A strong strategy is critical for progress, but strategy alone lacks effectiveness in a toxic or dull environment. The single factor common to successful change is that relationships improve. If relationships improve, things get better; if they remain the same or get worse, ground is lost. Thus, leaders must be consummate relationship builders with diverse people and groups—especially with people different than themselves. This is why emotional intelligence is equal to or more important than having the best ideas (Fullan, 2001). In Africa, there is a single word that expresses a deep philosophy of togetherness, recognition, and respect. *Ubuntu* (a Zulu word) can be translated to, "I am because we are," and we embraced this ideal in many ways at AISJ to build a culture of equity, inclusivity, and connectedness in the school. As leaders, we are the key culture builders who inspire our schools.

The best leaders are sense makers who provide clarity and coherence. They provide a compass that guides the way forward. Schools are extraordinarily complex organizations, and it is not always easy to see how the pieces fit together (Wheatley, 2006). Complex organizations inherently generate overload, fragmentation, and nonlinearity (Fullan, 2001). People, no matter their role, are inspired by an increasing understanding of how their work fits into the greater purpose, how each person makes a positive difference, and leaders need to explicitly connect the dots for everyone. Calling out and celebrating the connections of the system brings clarity and coherence to the complexity of a school.

"If you don't know where you're going, you'll end up someplace else." – Yogi Berra

Students learn deeply, educators are inspired, and everyone in the school community thrives when we are focused on our purpose, we stay true to our stated beliefs, and our shared vision is realized through thoughtful planning, sound implementation, reflection, and continuous improvement. Without a direction to follow and no educational GPS, we become less effective and stagnant. Without knowing where to go and how to get there - without a compass or a North Star - ultimately, we are lost.

Even though I was drifting in the sea without an engine or a GPS, I determined which way was north by the beautiful bright shining star above me. The Caribbean trade winds come out of the east, and they were blowing exceptionally strong that night. My boat was moving quickly through the water from the strong power of the wind, and fortunately I was headed toward land. My propeller wouldn't turn, but I figured out how to influence the direction I was heading by turning the lower unit of the engine, as well as using a paddle as a makeshift rudder. I really wasn't that far from land, and eventually I figured out the general direction of my home from several points of light on the horizon that were familiar landmarks. I saw a paper lantern, powered by a candle, emerging from the shoreline; I knew where it came from, and then I knew exactly where I was going. Magically, perhaps even divinely, after many hours, I got there.

Drucker, P. (1959). Work and Tools. Technology and Culture, 1(1), p. 28.

Fullan, M. (2001). Leading in a culture of change (1st ed.). Jossey-Bass.

Kotter, J. (2008). A sense of urgency (1st ed.). Harvard Business Press.

Olverson, T. (2015). Vision: How it's misunderstood and why heads need it. RG175, rg175.com/blog/57.

Schaar, J. (1981). Legitimacy in the modern state. Transaction Publishers.

Senge, P. (2006). The fifth discipline: The art & practice of the learning organization. (Revised & updated). Doubleday.

Sinek, S. (2011). Start with why: How great leaders inspire everyone to take action. Illustrated, Portfolio.

Wheatley, M. (2006). Leadership and the new science: Discovering order in a chaotic world (3rd ed.). Berrett-Koehler Publishers.

About Dr. Jeremy Moore

Jeremy Moore currently serves as the Director of the American International School of Johannesburg. With 25 years of experience as an educator and leader, Dr. Moore was a teacher, and also a Principal, at the Elementary, Middle and High School levels before becoming the Director at Cayman International School, where he served for a decade. Jeremy is a member of the Common Ground Collaborative advisory council, focused on reframing and bringing clarity to our understanding of learning and schools. He is also a member of the Middle States Association International Schools Accrediting Committee as well as multiple other organizations centered on international education. He has been a presenter at AASA, AAIE, and numerous other conferences, Board member of the AASA organization, and President of the Cayman Private Schools Association before moving to Africa. Dr. Moore is an alumnus of the Klingenstein Heads program at Columbia University, and he earned his Doctorate from the University of Florida. Jeremy likes to focus on 'what's right with the world', building community and positive culture in schools.

4

Understanding of Each Other

Mission, Vision, and Core Values

Dr. Mary Ashun

My father called me early one morning, asking a question that sounded simple: "What is school culture?"

I had no doubt that I knew the answer, but I honestly had never tried to explain it to an 85-year-old man who had been an educator several decades ago.

"This is when a school's mission, vision, and core values are easily recognized, Dad."

"But what does that really mean?"

I decided to answer him by giving him an example that popped right into my head because the event had just happened.

"During the Easter Holidays, four staff members decided on their own to visit one of the most deprived regions of the country to offer teaching and learning support to the teachers and administrators of the school. I had no hand in that. I did not seek out the opportunity; I did not direct them to do it, and my entire contribution to it on the surface was to say "yes" to them when they first approached me with their intent. Giving approval for them to do this was a no-brainer. They had seen a need. They were equipped to deliver support to address that need and they gave their time, at their own cost, to deliver the service."

"Why did they do that?"

"I think they are living out our mission, vision, and core values, Dad."

"But I don't recall anything in your mission and vision statements that talks about serving the needs of the underprivileged."

Does anyone else get the third degree at 7 o'clock in the morning by a parent? I realized if I didn't wake up properly, I really wouldn't be worthy of the title Head of School!

"Our vision, *Dear Father* (this said with emphasis), includes producing 'responsible global citizens.' We sense the needs around us and act accordingly. Our mission is to 'instill an understanding of each other,' and once we can do that, serving the needs of others becomes a matter of course. Emanating from these guiding statements will be a strategic plan and for our most recent one (2017–2022), one of our five goals was to 'Make Impact in Our Community Through Service.' This is exactly what our four staff members were doing. They demonstrated what we value, and when what we value is so palpable, it is easy to say that it is our school culture."

There was a very brief silence.

"That is wonderful. Now how do you find people who do that every single day?"

"Can we talk about that next time, Dad?"

Crafting mission, vision, and core value statements is a difficult task. Ours took months of careful, respectful discussion. What do we value? Why do we value it? Is it critical for us to make it a core value? Why? Why not? The mission statement is really about what you want to do. I often hear a *Star Trek*–like voice saying, "What is your mission, Captain?" The ever-capable Captain Kirk would respond, "To go where no man has gone before," and this sounded very strong, focused, and confident. A mission statement should be very bold, even a tad egotistical. It must make someone say (perhaps not too loudly): "Really? You seriously think you could do that?"

Our vision statement should be our way of saying that when we have gone "where no man has gone before"; we will look like what this vision statement says. Our vision statement will therefore give us some good hints about our core values— these are distinctive characteristics that remain when the fluff is shaved off.

My father's questioning was very timely since I was to write this chapter and highlight my experiences after leading the Ghana International School (GIS) for eight years. I was born and raised for part of my latter childhood in Ghana. I left for university in the United Kingdom, and at the time I wasn't sure I would be back given the political instability and economic hardships the country was experiencing. As I grew older, I realized how much I felt like coming back to my roots. In the Akan culture (one of the tribal groups), a symbol known as *Sankofa* is often used to demonstrate the "going back" phenomenon. Translated literally, *Sankofa* means "go back and fetch it," implying you may have left something behind. Returning to Ghana from Canada in the fall of 2014, I felt like I was coming back to fetch something after being away for almost 30 years.

I am the principal and head of school of GIS, an elite day private school in the capital city of Accra. I care for 1,300 students, ranging from ages 3–18, with the support of over 350 staff made up of academic and nonacademic members on our two campuses (Primary and Secondary), which are a hive of activity every single day of the school year! As can be expected, as people work and learn together, there is potential for issues to arise and some, if not dealt with, can turn into conflicts.

One early memory of mine is when the human resources manager came to see me in my office to share the news that a beloved staff member had suddenly been hospitalized. He had woken up blind. This was quite a shock to me since I had never heard of anyone experiencing such a thing. He was now safely being attended to in the hospital. I immediately sprang into action and suggested we send some flowers and a card. The HR manager looked hesitant.

"Is there a problem?" I asked.

"Yes, ma'am."

"Could you share what's wrong?"

She paused briefly and then proceeded with some caution. I noticed all of this and wondered what was so profoundly difficult to share with me about the suggestion I had made.

"Well, ma'am, could I suggest something else?"

"Yes, of course. Why not flowers and a card?"

"They are lovely, don't get me wrong. But here, people would prefer cooked food or fruits and vegetables, to flowers and a card . . . something more practical, I think."

Oh dear, I thought to myself. *Why didn't I think of that?* I felt I was blushing and quickly thanked her for the suggestion, and she left to implement the idea. I recall slumping in my seat in the office like a rag doll, wondering why my mind did not go there. Is it that I don't care as much? Is it that I have forgotten to consider the basic needs of people? The introspection continued for longer than it should have and hit me where it hurt a lot: at my identity. Here I was, feeling like I was Ghanaian in my core with North American experiences and knowing that most Ghanaians would have thought the same as my HR manager, which meant I wasn't Ghanaian enough, if there was such a thing. The saga continued for well over 18 months, since the gentleman never recovered enough to come back to work but had to resign from his position at the school. Each time we had to determine how best to support him, the issue of policies and how much we must align our actions with policy kept coming up. I would often find myself on the opposite side of my managers as I tried to convince them to work strictly with laid-down policies. Each time, I would be reminded that relationship dictated that we bear policy in mind but not let it destroy one of our core values: **Understanding of Each Other**.

Ghanaians are relationship people. People you've never known before can be referred to as Uncle or Auntie on first meeting. When you meet someone and they ask you how you are, they will often add "and how are my children?" in asking after *your* children. Essentially, your children are their children, and you need to accept that. There is a sense of community in many aspects of Ghanaian life. Although many families no longer live in rural areas, urbanity has not eroded what relationship means to most Ghanaians. As a school head, some staff refer to me as "mummy"; and while that irked me a whole lot at first (*do I look that old to be a 40-year-old woman's mummy?*), I have now seen it as a sign of relationship and respect. I was surprised to learn that funerals are attended by anyone who knew anyone connected to the dearly departed. At many funerals, the family "cut a cloth," meaning they design and purchase a particular cotton fabric designed locally and wear it in the design of their choice as a show of relationship. In the last couple of years, I've discovered that when they say the "family" is "cutting a cloth," they mean anyone who considers themselves family. And because relationship can mean as little as living in the same town as someone else, it is not unusual to attend a funeral and find that most individuals are wearing the same cotton fabric - and are therefore considered family. What this means for me as a school leader is that I have to set up boundaries that are realistic, manageable, and not draconian.

On the one hand, I cannot attend every funeral of someone related to one of the 350+ people I work with, but I cannot also act as if we are not "family." Therein lies the conundrum of respecting the culture's values. As a leader, everyone is looking up to you to lead in every way, regardless of how unrealistic it is. And how I have managed to navigate this is by setting up clear boundaries right at the beginning and making sure that the boundary setting does not indicate a lack of desire to connect and build a relationship. I strive to do that - from the school gardeners to the janitors to the canteen service providers and our teachers - I am present. With every opportunity I get, I constantly indicate my willingness to have them meet with me and I follow through on issues. While it takes longer to allow these actions to show that as a leader you care, it is still a sure way of letting people know that your relationship with them is very important to you. I am sure they would still be thrilled to see me at the funeral of their loved one, but I think they know that if I do not show up it is not because I have no relationship with them.

In our school's mission statement, we firmly state that we want "To provide an internationally diverse school experience that instills an understanding of each other, promotes holistic development, life skills and learning through a rigorous curriculum that meets international standards." Our school subscribes to an accreditation cycle that is rigorous to say the least. The Council of International Schools and the New England Association of Schools and Colleges (our two accreditors) have been of immense support in helping us benchmark our practice. At the same time the process is tedious, it is incredibly rewarding. These two organizations have accredited us since 2008, and we take pride in displaying their logos after a successful evaluation. At their most recent visit in 2018, the accrediting team - made up of evaluators from both organizations - expressed a keen desire to understand why we did not seem as bothered as they were with what they called "large" class sizes. I was not surprised. In North America, where the bulk of my teaching experience has been, I have never experienced a class size of over 25 in an elite private school, but, this is not unusual here at GIS. I asked them what "large" meant to them. Is it just a number? Is it based on a comparison? Does research support it? Many educators will attest that the jury is out on what the best class size is. It is dependent on so many factors - chief of which seems to be the capacity of the teacher to engage with a certain number of children in a satisfactory manner. The visiting evaluators had noted that each of our Primary classrooms had what we called a "junior teacher." This teacher is being mentored by the classroom teacher, one we call a "master teacher." Junior teachers are trained and certified at Teachers College in their assigned developmental age level. They could handle their classes and, in fact, during their four-year training tenure in our school, they can increase contact time with our students as the classroom teacher cedes some aspects of management of the class to them semester after semester. What this means is that our teacher–student ratio is not really 1:25; it is more like 1:12, which is a ratio the evaluators were expecting in a school of this stature. I also added that apart from providing more engagement for our students, we were also opening up our learning spaces to trainee teachers, increasing the capacity of teacher learners and contributing to aspects of teacher training that the country badly needed help with. As a school privileged to operate in the country of Ghana, sharing our resources, especially our human resources, is one of our goals clearly outlined in our strategic plan. Our approach to class sizes may not be what other schools in other jurisdictions may be used to, but this does not make it imperfect.

The visiting evaluators also wondered how truancy was not an issue for us, and even students in the Secondary School could not be found loitering during a free period! We work hard at maintaining a disciplined campus, I explained, and are fortunate to have many parents who support us in this endeavor. Children are reminded daily what they are in school for, and the responsibility of the privilege they have been given. They have a responsibility to their parents and to society to make the best use of the time allotted for lessons, be they chemistry, sports, or music lessons. Our ability to manage larger numbers than normal in another jurisdiction is due to support from the community. Our expectations for students within the learning environment are the same that their parents and community have of them. As a leader, one must understand the context within which one operates and use that context to find what works best in the school environment. Reading articles on what excellent schooling should be is a great exercise. Taking every idea and thought, lock, stock and barrel without considering one's local context is not wise.

Finally, our vision to be "A highly respected school, locally and internationally recognized, providing excellent education in a multicultural setting that produces responsible global citizens" is one I keep revisiting. What is currently niggling me is the word *multicultural* since it implies that there should be quite a lot of cultural diversity in the school. Many people would confess, however, that we lean mostly toward trying to achieve racial diversity because that is often more visible than cultural diversity. Some have implied that if we are not culturally or racially diverse, we are not excellent or some such thought. It niggles because demographics are changing so fast all around the world. In Ghana and much of Africa, the burgeoning middle class has meant that elite schools that were only able to attract expatriates and a handful of well-placed locals are now bursting on their application portals with interest from locals who can pay. How can we express our diversity in other ways when what everyone sees first is color? I once had a visit by a European father whose company had relocated him to work in Ghana. He noted our curriculum was British and was pleased with that. He must have spoken to others and been assured of the environment for teaching and learning so he reached out and booked a tour. On finishing the tour, he turned to me and exclaimed: "I saw fewer non-Ghanaian children than I expected. Why are there so few foreigners here?"

I explained that the children he'd seen and thought were Ghanaian were probably Nigerian, Kenyan, South African, and perhaps Burkinabe and racial mixes he would never guess in a million years. They may have looked like Ghanaians with all the shades of dark, but their cultures were different from Ghanaian culture in ways they would deem unique. The man did not enroll his children because he wondered how competent we were to deliver the curriculum, and he felt his children might not fit in. I mulled over this since for many elite schools outside Africa, the homogeneity of the student body, leaning toward Caucasians, has never been a reason for thinking the school would not be excellent. Since that experience, I've always asked those non-Ghanaians of Caucasian descent and who choose to enroll their children at GIS why they do so. Why do they have confidence in our ability to deliver world-class education, and why do they choose to place their children with others who do not look like them? Many of their answers boil down to this:

> I have been given an opportunity to raise my children with people who don't look like them, may not think like them, eat different foods, and perhaps worship differently from them. What a fantastic opportunity to have them grow up understanding how uniquely different and special we all are. And, you're accredited by reputable organizations!

In such a divided world, there are fewer and fewer opportunities to create environments that draw us closer to an understanding of each other and so while our vision niggles me, the challenge for me and all school leaders is how we move our school communities closer and closer to accepting that we must change with the times and help children to do the same.

In thinking through the mission, vision, and core values of our school, I would like to end with one of the verses from our school song:

May we go out from this our school

In the glory of our youth

And be prepared to live our lives

With courage, honour and truth

And as the days pass by one by one

May we be made to see

The greatest gift in life must be

Understanding of Each Other

About Dr. Mary Ashun

Dr. Mary Ashun is the Principal of Ghana International School and prior to this, she taught and led schools in Canada for several years. Mary lectured at Redeemer University (Ontario) teaching and supervising pre-service and in-service teachers. Mary holds a BSc from Univ. of East London (UK), a B.Ed. from Univ. of Toronto, a Ph.D from SUNY Buffalo, NY and is a Klingenstein Fellow of The School of Education, Columbia University in NY. She is a Board Member of the Association of Internationally Certified Schools (ASICS) in Ghana, the Association of International Schools in Africa (AISA) and Chair of the Advisory Board of Mastercard Foundation's *Young Africa Works*. Mary writes novels, short stories, and musicals, and most recently in March 2022, executive-produced a student adaptation of Nobel Laureate Wole Soyinka's play, *Death & The King's Horseman*. Mary is married to Joe and they have three adult sons.

5

Enhancing Professional Capacity in Schools: The Importance of a Professional Growth and Accountability Framework

Professional Capacity of Educators

Lee Fertig

Linda, a third-grade teacher at an international school, had been teaching for more than thirty years. As an experienced teacher, she believed she might be able to slightly tweak her professional practice in some small ways but that she would not benefit from any sort of significant shift in how she approached instruction and assessment. Her sense was that she already knew most of the art and science of teaching. A year later, as she engaged with her craft with novelty, creativity, and risk-taking, she reflected on how wrong she was to initially think she could not learn that more. She was now enjoying tremendous inspiration and renewed vigor in her practice.

A young and relatively inexperienced middle school math teacher, Olivia effectively engaged most of her students and ensured they were successful learners. Unfortunately, she struggled to collaborate with other teachers on her team due to an intransience in approaching team-teaching and an unwillingness to work with others on cross-moderating common assessments (both key features at the school). Grudgingly accepting guidance and new expectations from her supervising administrator, Olivia set out to work on these identified areas for improvement. Now, she works well with other teachers and facilitates powerful professional collaboration among teachers on a team that she leads.

Daniel, an experienced high school history teacher at an international school, was well respected by his students for his content knowledge and passion for the subject. But after several school administrators and an instructional coach finally convinced him that his students were suffering from not having enough learner agency in his classes, he agreed to try some new student-centered instructional strategies if he could be assured of regular, constructive feedback and sufficient support from others. Within months of working with an instructional coach, Daniel had substantially increased the number of tools in his teacher toolkit. Students reported having much more ownership of the activities in class and, in turn, were more engaged in the learning process.

What did Linda, Olivia, and Daniel have in common to significantly improve their professional practice? They all had access to a research-based and well-implemented framework for professional growth that was enthusiastically endorsed by their respective schools. They were able to actively embrace a disposition of lifelong learning by being immersed in school cultures that emphasized continuous improvement and self-accountability for learning.

With more than thirty years of school leadership experience in eight schools in five different countries on four continents, I cannot help but agree with the primary research finding of McKinsey & Company in their 2007 report, *How the World's Best-Performing School Systems Come Out on Top*: "The quality of an education system cannot exceed the quality of its teachers" (Barber & Mourshed, 2007). Much of this report focuses on the critical importance of getting the right people into the teaching profession and developing them into effective instructors. Even that organization's 2010 follow-up report, *How the World's Most Improved School Systems Keep Getting Better*, highlights the role of professional staff in schools, emphasizing the necessity to continually shape their practice through growth-oriented frameworks that embed peer collaboration and innovative ideation (Barber et al., 2010). In short, the professional capacity of school personnel appears to be a driving force in a school community's aspirations to fulfill its mission and vision boldly and effectively.

My experience in independent, international, and public schools confirms that school leadership needs to be intentional in prioritizing this professional growth framework if it is going to yield the desired effect. Simply assuming that faculty and staff will grow and develop in this way without any sort of system that holds them accountable to continually improve is not sufficient. School employees, on the academic and operational side of the organization, need to understand the research for such a framework, be supported with practical strategies that align with this research foundation, and have access to an organizational culture that explicitly and visibly values the concept of professional growth and accountability for learning. I explore each of these areas a bit further in the following sections.

The Research

In the past few decades, we have come a long way in terms of understanding how individuals learn and develop. Significant advancements in brain research, cognitive science, and psychology have provided new insights into how best to propel learning - not only in children but in adults as well. Much of the recent research on faculty and staff growth in schools derives directly from this new body of empirical literature. However, school leadership does not always embrace the evidence-based recommendations regarding professional growth and accountability in schools due to insufficient awareness of the research base, cultural challenges within their organizations, or simply inertia due to competing demands or lack of interest. So, unfortunately, archaic and ineffective approaches of appraising school personnel using inauthentic checklists that do not facilitate any meaningful reflection about professional practice continue to persist and play a large role in our efforts to enhance capacity in those who work in schools. In this section, I will briefly describe some of the key elements of the research that should be used to drive professional growth and accountability in schools with the hope that it can serve as an impetus for others to develop systems that are more aligned with what we know about adult learning.

Starting Assumption

Although we all make staff recruitment mistakes every now and then, most school leaders in international and private schools have the autonomy and know-how to make fairly good hiring decisions. Regardless of content expertise, skill set, and overall experience, we tend to identify, recruit, and hire professionals who have the disposition to continuously improve. Indeed, those who seek to continually improve performance and reflect upon their own practice have the professional disposition needed to be an effective teacher or staff member in a school (Purdue University, 2021). At times, we inaccurately assess this critically important attitude within the interview process but, more often than not, those we employ genuinely want to grow and improve in their practice. Then, why use an evaluative system that assumes they are not interested in ongoing learning? Many employee appraisal systems in schools use a static and reductionist model of professional performance rather than a dynamic approach to continuous improvement, one that leverages the inherent growth mindset found in so many school faculty and staff.

If indeed the large majority of those who work in our schools embrace a learning mindset, then the way they are expected to hold themselves accountable for learning (their own learning and that of those they serve) should be anchored in self-driven professional inquiry framed by the school's mission, vision, and learning principles. Teachers and staff members should be invited to share their own ideas on how they want to grow and develop, and be asked to articulate how they believe this will positively impact their professional practice. Of course, there are always a few who may need a little more prescriptive focus based on previous performance appraisals, but the majority of those who work in our schools should have the agency to at least cocreate their own professional learning goals, just as we emphasize in the sphere of student learning.

Structure and Process

Much of the recent research on professional growth and evaluation strongly suggests that there should be frequent opportunities for reflective dialogue with supervisors and others. Ongoing reflection, framed by a clearly defined continuum or rubric, appears to be much more effective in spurring professional growth than infrequent classroom visits and other detached observations. Marzano and Toth (2013) highlight the need to consider multiple accurate, data-rich measures of teacher performance and student growth, for example, to ensure meaningful self-reflection and evaluation takes place. Marshall (2013) also proposes a much broader framework for supervision and evaluation, one that enlists school personnel themselves to own accountability for learning, rather than cede responsibility for this to principals and other school leaders who too often use infrequent classroom visits, analysis of standardized test scores, and other externally driven measures of performance. Even human resource professionals in the private sector are now accepting the research that external feedback tends to decrease motivation, whereas reflective conversations around performance and constructive feedback focused on one's own goals tend to increase motivation, nurture that inherent growth mindset so many employees have, and retain talented and committed employees (Rodsevich, 2016). In short, ongoing discourse centered around one's own objectives and embedded in purposeful reflection is the best approach to build professional capacity in all school personnel. Of course, this must be grounded in the school's specific context, and it benefits from others' external validation, but the primary onus of professional growth should be intrinsic.

Standards and Indicators

However, this type of purposeful dialogue does not always arise on its own. Often, school personnel need a framework with a finite number of standards so they can reflect, share, and aspire to improve professional practice. Marzano and Toth (2013) emphatically criticize the use of narrow and artificial value-added measures (VAMs) and instead recommend multiple broader measures of growth and development. In many ways, this is no different than what we expect teachers to use with children in the classroom: standards, indicators, and rubrics that get to the heart of what we want them to learn. Why not adopt this same research-based approach with adults as we strive to build and sustain professional capacity? It is this feature of a highly effective growth and accountability framework that serves as the core of improvement in professional practice, a point to which I now turn.

The Practice

An effective framework for professional growth and accountability will require attention, nurturing, and resourcing if it is going to be beneficial. However, its structure can be quite simple. Three key elements need to be included and aligned for the system to have a sustainable impact over time, both for individual employees and the organization as a whole.

Standards

A school first needs to identify a small number of domains that it believes are the most important to be a successful teacher or staff member in that community. These domains can be articulated as broad-based standards, each of which can be more fully described in a continuum with supporting indicators at each level. At one international school where I worked, we developed four such standards that reasonably aligned with Charlotte Danielson's four domains of teaching responsibility but more aptly fit the specific context (Danielson, 2007, p. 26).

1. Design and deliver relevant student-centered instruction and assessment.
2. Create a student-centered classroom based on the school's learning principles.
3. Purposefully reflect and act upon pertinent learning evidence and model this for others.
4. Empower oneself and others to collaborate around improving student learning.

Each standard included a finite number of specific indicators which, in turn, were unpacked through four different levels on the continuum:

- Highly effective and able to model for others
- Effective
- Beginning
- Does not meet standard

This approach achieved several important design features in the framework. First, the school could clearly and visibly articulate what it deemed most important in professional practice. This in and of itself was a very positive exercise to engage in as it brought all employees together around a shared purpose. Second, the continuum and its specific indicators guaranteed that the process and reflection to be used for professional growth was evidence-driven. Faculty and nonteaching staff were expected to compile evidence about their professional practice and assess it using the rubric itself, thereby moving away from generalizations and overly subjective self-assessments. Finally, this continuum of standards and supporting indicators enabled each school employee to transparently share their self-assessments with others in the community if they wanted to. They could visibly share their reflections about their professional practice with their supervisor, colleagues, coaches, mentors, and even students if desired. As with many new initiatives in an international school setting, there was initially some reticence and resistance to the idea of using a common set of standards for all faculty and staff. However, once employees understood the growth-oriented nature of these standards and they directly experienced increased agency, improved efficacy, and heightened student engagement in the learning process, this skepticism quickly dissipated.

Growth Record

To capture ongoing self-assessment and reflection, a teacher or staff member needs to maintain a personal growth record that can be shared with others as part of the reflective journey. At one school I worked at, we furnished everyone with a suggested template, a collaborative Google document that could easily be accessed and updated. In another school, I encouraged employees to come up with their own mechanism for tracking their professional growth and continuous improvement. Examples of these platforms included personal websites, blogs, Twitter feeds, LinkedIn profiles, and journals. Regardless of the specific platform, all growth records were required to consider the following data elements:

- Self-assessment related to the standards and supporting indicators of the growth continuum.
- A summary of observational feedback from school leaders, colleagues, and others.
- For teachers, an analysis of student learning data and evidence of how this is being used to guide planning and teaching.
- A summary of feedback from students and/or those we interact with and serve in the community, along with evidence of how this is being used to inform professional practice.

Teachers and staff members were also encouraged to include evidence related to peer collaboration, coaching cycles, and mentoring in their growth records.

These growth records need to prioritize function over formality. They need to serve the main objective of capturing purposeful reflection that is timely and grounded in pertinent evidence. There also should be a collaborative feature to the platform so that others can contribute to the individual's ongoing dialogue about their journey of continuous improvement.

Feedback

In addition to learning and process data that are included in the growth record, evidence that summarizes others' perceptions about the individual's professional capacity is tremendously helpful. Teachers should be encouraged to solicit input from their students in developmentally appropriate ways. Parents can be surveyed to ascertain their assessment of how well the teacher is facilitating learning. Colleagues and others can be asked to constructively reflect upon how well they are doing as a professional.

In some ways, this type of feedback, even though it tends to be perceptual data, is one of the most important features of a professional growth and accountability framework. Working in schools is a social endeavor and, as such, we strive to effectively serve those who expect certain things from us as teachers, staff members, and leaders. A large part of holding ourselves accountable in a school community is making sure we not only advocate for ourselves but that we also empower those around us to be their best. Regularly collecting feedback from others with whom we interact, summarizing this data, and then reflecting upon how this evidence supports their growth can be incredibly powerful, yet it is rarely engaged in as a key feature of building professional capacity in school personnel.

In my role as head of school (director, superintendent, etc.), I always commit to soliciting feedback from a large swath of the school community, even in my first year at a school. I have even brought together members of the search committee that originally recommended my hiring to help me process feedback on my professional practice. In addition to this being a wonderful way of gauging how my transition into the new community is progressing, it publicly and unambiguously models for others the importance of capturing this type of feedback in our efforts to continuously improve in holding ourselves accountable for the job we are being asked to do. As an example, at one school this feedback uncovered the community's need for me to make my thinking and decision-making more visible so that they better understood my overall leadership approach. I used this input to create additional opportunities for informal dialogue which, in turn, enabled me to explain my rationale clearly and transparently for the actions I was taking as a school leader, something I might not have done so regularly if it were not for this feedback.

The Culture

"We hired you because we thought you were good, not because we thought you were perfect. We are all here to get better, and the only way we will get better is to make mistakes, reveal our limitations, and support each other to overcome them" (Kegan & Lahey, 2016, p. 38).

All our best efforts in building professional capacity of school personnel, as strategic and intentional as they may be, are for naught if the structure and process used are not buoyed by a genuine culture of professional growth. Ironically, schools often do not benefit from an empowering culture of learning, one in which all community members, including faculty and staff, are encouraged to take risks, and amply supported as they seek higher levels of self-accountability. The leadership job of culture shaping is foundational to an impactful professional growth framework. But *reculturing*, as Fullan (2011, p. 18) so succinctly indicated, is "never a checklist, always complexity."

School leaders need to incessantly assess, shape, and steward cultural change with all school personnel around professional growth and accountability. In addition to leading by example by soliciting feedback on my own performance as previously indicated, I spend a lot of time engaging in Bolman and Deal's humanistic, structural, and political frames of leadership (2021) as well to build a culture of continuous improvement and self-accountability in professional practice. I actively lead the implementation of the framework myself, making sure that people know how committed I am to this work and how important I believe it to be. I use a growth record myself and reflect upon evidence with other school leaders and trustees. I explicitly demonstrate vulnerability in my own growth journey and highlight when I have been both successful and unsuccessful in holding myself accountable. All of this revolves around a leader's key role in facilitating a positive culture, a necessary ingredient in the recipe of enhancing professional capacity in a school community. DuFour and Fullan (2013, p. 2) underscore the paradox of culture change: "It is absolutely doable, but it is also undeniably difficult." My experience, however, suggests that a leader should never shy away from this challenge, no matter how difficult it is, if they want to be successful.

The Leadership Lesson

Linda, Olivia, and Daniel are three professionals that I had the privilege of working with over the years who tremendously enhanced their practice because of a robust professional growth and accountability framework. One is now retired as a teacher but is often recruited to engage in instructional coaching with others. Another works at a graduate school of education, ensuring that teachers have access to pertinent and impactful educational research about their professional practice. The third continues to teach in an international school, often being identified as one of the students' favorite teachers. My hope and expectation are that all three look back upon their time using this framework as a moment in their career characterized by tremendous growth and professional development. I would like to think that my leadership in this realm was a contributing factor in their own professional journeys of continuous improvement.

There were many more who benefited in meaningful ways from this type of approach to professional growth, and even more who would have benefited if they had had the opportunity to continuously improve their practice with such a system. The leadership lesson in all of this is simple: School leaders must build a research-based professional growth and accountability framework regardless of context, provide concrete strategies that enhance professional practice within this framework, and prioritize culture shaping that supports this type of improvement-oriented discourse. A school will only be as good as those who work in it, so building professional capacity in all personnel is critically important in each and every school community.

Specifically, school leaders need to visibly model how to use this growth framework. They have the opportunity and responsibility to ensure it gets on and stays on top of the continuous improvement agenda of the school. And leaders must not be shy about celebrating significant improvements in professional practice stemming from the framework. These are the leadership strategies that constructively hold all of us accountable for learning in our communities.

It is important to note that all practitioners in a school community benefit from using a professional growth and accountability framework. Obviously, teachers must constantly strive to enhance student growth. Nonteaching staff members also have a responsibility to propel learning in themselves and for those with whom they interact. School leaders must embrace the notion of servant leadership and focus on how they best serve their constituents. Even school board members, often serving as volunteers, are encouraged to use a framework that consists of standards, growth records, and feedback mechanisms - all aligned and anchored in a clearly defined evidence-driven framework.

Schools are learning organizations. The professionals who work in the schools are expected to facilitate this learning. I strongly encourage us to empower every practitioner to hold themselves accountable for the learning. Providing them with the access, agency, and aspiration to do this is at the core of our leadership job.

Barber, M., ChiJioke, C., & Mourshed, M. (2010). How the world's most improved school systems keep getting better. McKinsey & Company.

Barber, M., & Mourshed, M. (2007). How the world's best-performing school systems come out on top. McKinsey & Company.

Bolman, L. G., & and Deal, T. E. (2021). Reframing organizations: Artistry, choice, and leadership (7th ed.). Jossey-Bass.

Danielson, C. (2007). Enhancing professional practice: A framework for teaching, 2nd ed. ASCD.

DuFour, R., & Fullan, M. (2013). Cultures built to last: Systemic PLCs at work. Solution Tree Press.

Fullan, M. (2011). Change leader: Learning to do what matters most. Jossey-Bass.

Kegan, R., & Lahey, L. L. (2016). An everyone culture: Becoming a deliberately developmental organization. Harvard Business School.

Marshall, K. (2013). Rethinking teacher supervision and evaluation: How to work smart, build collaboration, and close the achievement gap. Jossey-Bass.

Marzano, R. J., & Toth, M. D. (2013). Teacher evaluation that makes a difference: A new model for teacher growth and student achievement. ASCD.

Purdue University. (2021). Professional dispositions in education. Purdue Online. https://online.purdue.edu/blog/education/dispositions

Rodsevich, M. (2016). This is how Google redefines performance management. Talent Culture. https://talentculture.com/this-is-how-google-redefines-performance-management/

About Dr. Lee Fertig

Lee Fertig has served as a teacher and educational leader in eight schools in five countries on four continents. His career spans 30 years of leadership in schools (22 as Director / Head of School). Mr. Fertig was named a Klingenstein Heads of Schools Fellow at Teachers College, Columbia University. He has also taught as a course facilitator for the Principals' Training Center (PTC) for over a decade. Outside of his work in schools, Mr. Fertig has served as a trustee for the Council for the Advancement and Support of Education (CASE) and is a previous board member of the Association for the Advancement of International Education (AAIE), the Global Issues Network (GIN), and the Sao Paulo Education Foundation (SPEF).

6

The Importance of Intentionality: Unifying Expats and Locals in One Staff Culture

Professional Capacity of Educators

Dr. Audrey C. Menard

Imagine a school where the locally hired teachers spend non-classroom time with their peer group and the expat-hired teachers spend non-classroom time with their separate cohort. Tables at lunch self-segregate by language and type of contract. Imagine further, the operational staff and teaching assistants also keep to themselves, rarely interacting with even the locally hired teachers. Expat employees comprise the administration almost exclusively and take lunch with the English-speaking expats. Complaints by local employees about inequity in pay and benefits compared to expat pay packages rumble as a constant undertone. The administration puts tremendous energy and resources into recruiting, hiring, and retaining expat employees while essentially filling holes for local postings. Faculty meetings and staff communications occur only in English, despite—especially frontline staff - speaking only the national languages and dialects. School-sponsored social celebrations tend to feature a Western look and feel despite the non-Western national culture, while local staff hold their own private celebrations on and off campus. The concept of "international culture" has never been defined explicitly. Silos are woven deeply into the fabric of the school.

This true story exhibits typical challenges in the international education circuit. Beginning my tenure as head of this international school, these prevalent divisions concerned me. Before jumping into much-needed strategic planning and a mission refresh, I first needed to understand the community and seek to unify it. Initially, I learned as much as I could about the community and those who comprised it. I met with employees who self-selected into small groups or one-on-one, often requiring the support of an interpreter. Some of the smaller affinity groups felt more comfortable sharing their experiences thematically rather than by personal experience. I also surveyed the school community regarding culture and community in two or three languages. I looked at themes and created focus groups to explore concerns further. I analyzed external data including market trends for local and expat employees regarding salary and benefits. Finally, I practiced "management by walking around," at times letting me learn more through informal conversations than from formal data-gathering methods.

These first efforts yielded invitations for me to local celebrations, both in school and out. I made efforts to eat lunch with non-expats, despite feeling somewhat awkward and uncomfortable when conversations flowed in and out of their native language I stuck with it, knowing, as an expat myself, that I could not bring the school together without first making my own in-roads with host country employees. I updated our communications to include the local language and —through WhatsApp voice messages and additional meetings—to include those among our frontline staff who were not literate. I replaced some expat leadership with local supervisors and worked with them to change the culture. Once I understood the local context and local faculty and staff were included and informed, trust was built, and silo walls lowered. I knew my efforts were working because of the invitations I received, daily enthusiastic greetings from the local staff, and general comments of thanks for my efforts to help the community come together. Expat staff also benefitted from a richer school culture that incorporated local interests. I made this shift transparent and spoke openly about the need for unity. We re-envisioned the culture and community we wanted. We tied this to our mission and values. Morale improved and walls came down.

Twelve Lessons Learned

This case study summarizes years of work and oversimplifies the hard work this entails. Many of my successes were learned through error, often the hard way. In hindsight, I can share twelve lessons learned from my time at this school.

Lesson 1: A large contingent of the local community had been around for lengthy tenures. They had seen waves of expats come and go. New local staff initially developed what felt like rewarding relationships with the expats, only to have the more mobile expats leave and not keep in touch. In time, the local community learned to stop investing in these relationships too deeply, viewing expats as world explorers seeking exoticisms more than as desiring to embed in local culture with deep and lasting friendships. Expats, they felt, wanted to maximize the cursory experience of new sites, sounds, food, and customs during their limited tenures. Many locals told me they had tired of investing time in expats to just see them leave. It simply was not worth the effort. I could not begin knocking down walls without first understanding this important distinction.

Lesson 2: Recruiting the best talent available has always led priorities for international schools. We spent lots of money, time, and other resources traveling to job fairs, putting together competitive packages, developing exciting on-boarding programs, and legalizing all employees. We spent much time and effort coddling the expats by holding their hands through every step of the way as they moved through the culture shock curve. By contrast, filling local positions often meant perusing resumes for people with good English skills and high education regardless of good fit of experience to posting, or even hiring through friends and family connections. With efforts so laser-focused on expats, I learned that the locals felt excluded, undervalued, and taken for granted. They did not feel like they really mattered to the school.

Lesson 3: Leading international schools requires building relationships to gain access to critical information. I invested significant time to earn trust one person at a time. For local staff, I knew the language barrier often would interfere. I found individuals who could serve as interpreters whom the local community trusted with credibility and discretion. I learned that trusted interpreters and me meeting with them in small groups and/or one-on-one provided me with valuable information. Sometimes affinity groups were preferred, such as the cleaning ladies who wanted to meet with me as a group to share their common experience, or the local teachers with the school's longest tenures wanting to share common perspective on trends over time. On the other hand, many wanted to meet one-on-one with no interpreter to share confidential information. I met with all the expat staff as well, following the same methodology but without an interpreter. I felt it was important to treat every employee in as close to the same manner as possible. While time-consuming, I found that relationships and trust could develop among most employees, with the reward of deep insights into the community that I could not have obtained sitting at the desk in my office.

Lesson 4: At lunch time, I split my time between local hires and expat employees. Despite my poor skills in the local language, I made an effort to follow along and contribute as I could as they switched back and forth between English and their mother tongue. I felt awkward, uncomfortable, and even clueless. Sometimes I wondered if they saw me as an intruder. However, I knew I needed to model this behavior. Slowly, I began to feel welcomed. In time, some of the local hires would join me at an expat table. It was first those who spoke English fluently. Then others started to join knowing there was an interpreter in the mix. I worked hard to include them in the conversations. I wanted to eliminate as many of the barriers I felt in the other direction. I learned that you have to be willing to be uncomfortable, put yourself into the daily local context/experience, dive into the unknown, and embrace it. Local employees need to see your willingness to get to know them despite barriers. All employees saw my efforts to socialize as not favoring any particular group. The results paid big dividends.

Lesson 5: From surveys, focus groups, and one-on-one meetings, I learned that communication was a key issue internally. We hosted a culture hack that included two competing teams to explore campus communication challenges and to recommend solutions. Both teams were comprised of representatives of local and expat employees together, with multilingual staff serving as translators. At the end of the process, the teams shared their findings with the school community. We learned that communication only in English was a huge challenge for many. Furthermore, most school communication targeted only the teaching/academic staff. Our frontline workers often knew nothing about scheduled happenings at school. They were at best an afterthought. Additionally, we learned that we employed many illiterate staff. We created WhatsApp chats and communicated with them by voice message. However, even many local teaching staff struggled with the English-heavy verbal communication of meetings. We did not follow the very Sheltered Instruction Observation Protocol (SIOP) we asked our teachers to use in the classrooms with our English as an Additional Language (EAL) population. I learned that two-way communication must be offered in at least the host country language and English to ensure everyone is on the same page.

Lesson 6: Many people with whom I met doubted I would tackle their issues. I made clear that it would take time, but I would prioritize them. With each action accomplished, my credibility increased. One issue I uncovered related to another campus subgroup: the outsourced security team that operated with almost no collaboration with the school. For example, they received no advance notice of fire and lock-down drills and had no idea what was happening when they occurred. The school gave them no strategic direction, leaving them to operate the front gate and wander around the campus. They did not get invited to community gatherings. Using a trusted translator, I met with the head of the security guards and his second in command. They expressed gratitude for this opportunity to be acknowledged and included. I later discovered that the expat in charge of security had intentionally excluded them for reasons never explained to me. I began including the guards in communications, trainings, communicating directly via WhatsApp with the help of Google translate, and supporting them in other ways. Since we subcontracted them, we could not bonus them. Instead, we bought them seasonal uniforms and provided bountiful meat, produce, and pantry items for their families during certain holidays. Years after moving to my next school, they keep in touch with me and say prayers for my family. Treating people with care and acknowledging their humanity results in respect. I learned you must give more than lip-service to problems; you must tackle them strategically, so the staff knows you are serious about changing the culture. By doing so, your value and allegiance with the staff rise significantly.

Lesson 7: The difference in salary scales between locally hired and foreign teachers seems to be an unspoken issue in many schools. Salary scales at my school were not published for any staff member. Human Resources (HR) would use the "secret scale" and let people know their compensation package. This secrecy bred a lot of distrust among everyone. People claimed they worked out special deals. Local hires believed expats received tremendous benefits on top of higher salaries. They understood that some of this is normal, but the lack of transparency led to local hires feeling, once again, not valued by the organization. I learned the benefit to the entire staff community of making teacher salary schemes transparent for both expats and locals.

Moreover, administrations should follow these consistently. Creating ad hoc exceptions quickly becomes a slippery slope. Special arrangements undermine trust in schools. Expat and local hire teaching scales should have the same pay for the same work, making it easier for locals to appreciate the additional benefits received by the expats for things like school-paid expat payroll taxes, housing, shipping, flights, and so on.

Furthermore, schools can allow custom-created benefits by offering a menu approach tailored to the differing needs of local and expat employees. I learned that this transparency and standardization were mission critical to creating equality where possible to help two different pools of employees become one community. We were able to adopt these practices successfully.

Lesson 8: While diversity existed in the teaching staff, only expats comprised the school leadership. As I met with local hires, I discovered this was a barrier to local staff sharing concerns with the administration. Some expat leaders could not envision the diverse range of employee needs and interests beyond their own expat status. Their attitudes included thinking local employees were lucky to have jobs; they were "saving" local staff from their own country; and the benefit of hiring local employees was to staff with inexpensive labor. This was especially problematic for our frontline workers and our teaching assistants. Including local staff, not just expats, in leadership fosters care for the entire community. While some expats groused, the replacement of several expat administrators with local managers improved the information flow and the satisfaction of the employees in general. This allowed me to have a better handle on both the climate and the culture of the school (climate: the way it feels to a part of the school community; culture: the way we do things around the school).

Lesson 9: The leadership never considered school culture with intentionality. It was an ethereal concept. We felt more like roommates all coexisting in a shared space than in a symbiotic relationship. We did not seek to create a culture with a warm climate supporting all employees. We confronted prima facia problems reactively instead of addressing fundamental issues strategically. Seeking to bring substance to "international culture" in our vernacular, intentional community-wide effort yielded a greater impact on school climate than did letting exist a panoply of superficial conceptions. An international community is more than languages, passports, flags, festivals, and food. We wanted a school identity grounded on the richness of each person's unique identity. Instead of generalizing one-dimensional group traits, we sought to know each other personally. Unpacking this from our mission and values let our diversity enrich our community overall. Local staff reached out to the expats again, and expats left their comfort zones. Without defining and inculcating international culture expressly and intentionally to fit your school context, school culture devolves to be anything to anyone and nothing really to everyone.

Lesson 10: Having defined culture, I had to create opportunities for everyone to know each other outside of their self-created circles. This took many forms, each one planned and executed carefully. We scrapped some professional development work to focus on building relationships. For instance, we brought in some game experts for a fun and competitive field day with diverse teams that mixed staff. Through play, communication was easier, and teams' common goals (winning) were nonthreatening. Everyone laughed and bonded as they worked together to use the talents of the team to take on the field day challenges. We also started lunch time book groups, with books available in both English and the local language. During faculty meetings, we assigned seats to break people's seating cliques. We planned weekend social options for staff families to come for kickball, food, and fun, with teams again formed into diverse groups that created their own team names and attire. We hosted opportunities for expats to learn about the meanings, practices, and customs behind holidays and celebrations from local staff. Expats, as well, shared their personal backgrounds and customs. This underscored my learning that culture and community must be built and cared for intentionally through planned experiences. I learned the school's role in teaching expats about local culture, customs, holidays, expectations, religion, and more, emphasizing their status as guests in the host country.

Lesson 11: I also learned about hiring mission-appropriate expat staff. There are many reasons that expats choose the life of an overseas teacher. Some use teaching to fund their traveling adventures. Others really want to join a community and embrace their host country. We decided to change our hiring strategy to go after those who would embrace our definition of an international community and actively participate in it. We made those expectations clear starting in the interview process and found mission-appropriate teachers who came to our school with a congruent mindset. I learned that intentionally hiring expats with a strong desire to enrich their own lives professionally and personally through engaging with the local community also lowered the cultural silo walls.

Lesson 12: Finally, after living abroad in countries once occupied by foreign powers, I have learned to beware of vestiges of colonialism in the local culture. As a leader, I must keep in mind the impact of history on culture, as things an expat might never think of as offensive could be received that way by the local population. Be it English teatime, French cuisine, or schedules featuring American holidays, expats may need to check their enthusiasm for things that carry vestiges of a colonial past. While the nationals may appreciate some of the influences left in their country after independence, resentments can persist as well. I found the local population receives and understands things in a context different from mine and must navigate the consequent post-colonial love–hate relationship with diplomacy.

In summary, creating a singular and desirable culture in an international school requires understanding people, modeling desired behavior, creating clear vision and expectations, and ensuring opportunities to practice desired behaviors. I had to be very intentional and find courage to be vulnerable to break down the silos. Slowly, this strategic work succeeded in creating an environment that was comprehensively singular, positive, and truly international.

About Dr. Audrey C. Menard

Dr. Audrey C. Menard earned her undergraduate degree, summa cum laude, at Longwood University. She has an M.Ed. in Educational Administration from the University of Massachusetts, and completed her doctorate in education leadership, policy, and organization at Vanderbilt University.

Dr. Menard is a strong advocate for school reform and has traveled to schools across the U.S. and internationally to support her own professional research on how to reshape education in the 21st century. Among her varied accomplishments, Dr. Menard's efforts include improving school cultures, ensuring a student centered approach to guide all decision making; breaking down silos to create singular and aligned communities; development of dynamic and impactful strategic plans, in collaboration with Boards and school stakeholders; budget development and administration aligned to schools goals and mission; and developing documented manuals including policies, processes and procedures that ensure mission alignment throughout her schools.

Dr. Menard has diverse experience in both domestic and international school administration. She has served 11 years as a Head of School, 8 years as a MS and HS Principal, in addition to serving as an Assistant Principal and Mathematics teacher. She currently serves as Head of School at the International School of Panama in Panama City, Panama.

7

Building Professional Capacity Post-Pandemic: Three Lessons

Professional Capacity of Educators

Dan Yamasaki

During the pandemic, our school was closed for almost an entire year before we returned for five months with limited students on campus. We have been back to in-person schooling for the 2021–2022 school year but with many COVID-19 restrictions, which we are all familiar with. Adapting to new conditions and teaching environments has put an enormous burden on teachers. Schools now must balance the need for ongoing professional development (PD) with the limited time and energy teachers devote to this endeavor. Nevertheless, the COVID-19 pandemic, as tragic as it has been for so many people, has been a great teacher. This chapter will discuss three lessons learned from our attempts to build professional capacity during and after the pandemic: How we assessed teacher readiness, selected a high-leverage PD focus, and increased teacher agency in school PD.

I am the general director of Colegio Panamericano, in Bucaramanga, Colombia. As a medium-sized school of 780 students, coordination of PD falls on the leadership team with help from the lead teachers and department heads. It was apparent early in the pandemic that teachers were overwhelmed. This feeling lessened as we transitioned back to a hybrid instruction model and then back to in-person learning. Yet it was clear that the teachers' cups were full. Nevertheless, we felt it was critical to continue providing teachers with opportunities for focused professional growth, especially in our school's major initiative, STEAM education.

STEAM at Colegio Panamericano

Originating as an American policy response to increased global and workforce competitiveness 20 years ago, STEM education has been adopted by schools worldwide (Affouneh et al., 2020; Carter, 2017; Keratithamkul et al., 2020). Six years ago, Colegio Panamericano began implementing a school-wide STEAM program, integrating the areas of science, technology, engineering, arts and humanities, and math. The STEAM program at Panamericano is an inquiry-based pedagogy designed to develop future-ready students with the innovative mindsets and skills necessary to solve problems and succeed in an ever-changing world. Central to the STEAM program are integrated class projects that encourage students to see knowledge as interconnected and promote active learning and a problem-based approach to learning. In addition, the pedagogical skills and deep conceptual knowledge required to teach, plan, implement, and assess STEAM projects mean that robust PD structures must be in place.

STEAM Projects

Like many schools, when the pandemic hit Colombia, we shifted to a virtual learning model. Nevertheless, the STEAM instruction continued as teachers found creative ways to develop the curriculum, have students work collaboratively, and even exhibit student work for audiences through Zoom meetings. However, teacher surveys showed that 75% of STEAM teachers desired more PD, suggesting that teachers did not feel sufficiently prepared to plan and carry out high-quality STEAM projects. This lack of knowledge is a problem since teaching STEAM requires a deep understanding of the content areas of science, technology, engineering, arts and humanities, and math, which many teachers lack (Dan & Gary, 2018). Compounding this problem is teachers' limited energy as they continually adapt to new conditions and restrictions.

Impact of COVID-19

Even two years after the initial outbreak, COVID protocols that require modifications to schedules, programs, and school routines are still in place in many schools. COVID factors impact students, staff, and parents. Closing schools due to the pandemic meant teachers had to acquire new skills, materials, and pedagogical strategies, which placed enormous demands on teacher time (González & Bonal, 2021).

In the school year 2020–2021, newly hired Panamericano expatriate teachers were unable to enter the country, complicating attempts to onboard new staff. Turnover of expatriate staff increased by 20% over past years' averages at Panamericano. Furthermore, mental health inventories applied to teachers showed that long work hours and the inability to manage time demands were challenges. Forty percent of staff reported anxiety symptoms (e.g., loss of sleep, loss/increase of appetite). This situation had the potential to hamper any new initiative.

Lesson 1: Teacher Readiness

It is not surprising that teachers felt overwhelmed. Like educators worldwide, our teachers had to develop new skills to support their students' learning and social needs as students transitioned from virtual to hybrid and in-person environments. Learning these new skills, often through trial and error, taxed teachers' time and energy. Any additional PD on STEAM projects would need to be structured with a high level of consideration for the limited readiness of staff.

Assessing Readiness

Readiness refers to how the organization and individuals involved are collectively motivated and capable of participating in the change process (Holt & Vardaman, 2013). Assessing our staff's readiness by reviewing contextual factors, especially the pandemic's effect and impact on teacher time and cognitive resources, was crucial for structuring this year's PD. Time is a limited resource in schools. A survey applied to Panamericano teachers in May 2021 showed that time management was challenging while working under pandemic restrictions. Thirty-three percent of teachers selected time management as the number one most challenging aspect of their school day.

Section principals reported that faculty meetings typically used for collaboration are now used to update routines around arrival/dismissal, recess, and lunchtime to comply with new COVID safety protocols. Informal conversations with staff complemented survey data, which told us that they were spending much of their time and energy maintaining their students' physical safety and emotional well-being during this transition back to in-person school. Under the current conditions, we knew that moving forward with any PD would need to be sensitive to teacher time and be highly relevant to the instructional challenges they were facing in the classroom.

Addressing Readiness

To address this state of readiness, we decided to limit our PD efforts to one high-leverage practice this year. In Charles Duhigg's book, *The Power of Habit* (2014), he asserts that 40% of our actions are habits and certain habits are keystone habits. Keystone habits are those that generate other positive habits. Duhigg cites an Australian study on university students. Over eight weeks, students engaged in regular exercise showed a decrease in smoking, drinking, and caffeine consumption; an increase in healthy eating; and less stress, less spending, better nutrition, and more disciplined behaviors than the control group. This increased regulatory behavior meant subjects were more likely to continue exercising, generating a virtuous cycle. Focusing on STEAM project tuning would be our keystone habit that would be the catalyst for the teachers' growth.

Project Tuning

The list of skills that STEAM teachers need to master is extensive (Duschl & Bybee, 2014). For example, quality STEAM projects require teachers to engage in the project planning cycle. Our school has determined that the six elements of the planning cycle include create the problem (essential question), plan the project, tune the project, launch the project, exhibit student work, reflect on the project, then repeat for the next project. Considering teacher readiness levels, we could not expect teachers to become literate in each element of the project planning cycle all at once. So instead of trying to sow a mile wide and an inch deep, we focused on one area: project tuning.

Project tuning is when teachers present their STEAM project plans to a group of teacher colleagues, often from similar grade levels. The colleagues offer valuable feedback on making the project more robust. Critical practices such as these encourage professional collaboration (Agarwal & Agarwal, 2016), offer spaces for reflection, and leverage the collective experience of several teachers to promote professional growth (Kilpatrick & Fraser, 2019).

Focusing on one element for PD allowed us to communicate expectations for teachers, increasing readiness. On our first PD day of the year, we gathered the entire staff and launched the year's PD initiative. I outlined our approach, timeline, and teacher expectations around project tuning. Experienced STEAM teachers would be required to present all their projects for tuning and sign up to critique a project at least once per quarter. Less experienced teachers would be encouraged to submit at least one project per semester for tuning and voluntarily critique a colleague's project.

In the complex landscape of international school leadership, clarity is sometimes elusive; however, clearly communicating the PD vision and what will be expected of staff can lead to positive attitudes toward the initiative and increase receptiveness, openness, and commitment to change (Napier et al., 2017; Rafferty et al., 2013). Despite the limited time, teachers were able to see the relevance of this PD opportunity, understand their commitment to the effort, and engage in the collaborative learning that is fundamental to addressing teacher hesitancy. Successful change requires the interdependence of individuals and is contingent on collective attitudes (Holt & Vardaman, 2013). The virtuous cycle started spinning!

Lesson 2: Shifting Away from a Workshop-Based PD

Travel restrictions during the pandemic meant that we would have to rethink our typical model of workshop-based PD. Over the years, Panamericano has developed partnerships with international organizations to provide training on STEAM projects for our staff. Each year the school would host a two-day institute for all staff on elements of project planning, assessing, or integrating different curricular areas or STEAM competencies. But unfortunately, travel restrictions froze any external expert from visiting Colombia. Although there are still plenty of workshops and conferences taking place in an online medium, we took advantage of this moment to rethink the workshop-based approach and utilize the skills of our staff and their disposition to share.

Workshop-based PD assumes that teacher growth is linear and that one-off teacher workshops lead to a change in classroom practices. However, the literature on PD shows that the workshop-based PD by itself is not sufficient. Professional development must be contextualized in teachers' daily work to be impactful (Castro Superfine & Li, 2014; Guskey, 2009). Furthermore, promoting collaborative practices and leadership involvement generates better outcomes (Guskey, 2003; Hilton et al., 2015). Researchers found that purposefulness in program structure targeted outcomes and empirically validated theories of learning yield better PD results (Guskey, 2003; Yoon et al., 2007). The one-off PD workshops model does little to impact students' results. Only when the PD is continuous and contextualized does it positively affect student outcomes (Yoon et al., 2007).

A Different Model for Teacher Growth

If workshop-based PD is ineffective, what PD models show better results? One of the models that has the potential to provide more relevant, collaborative, and continuous PD is an interconnected model for professional growth (Clarke & Hollingsworth, 2002). In the context of professional growth, learning occurs in an environment where teachers are encouraged to enact new strategies and reflect on their impact. Learning does not come from sitting in a workshop but from trying the new strategy and reflecting on its impact. The workshop has its place, but its purpose is to provide new information, skills, or stimulus for teacher growth.

Teacher growth emerges from the enactment and reflection between these different domains:

- External domain: New information or stimulus
- Personal domain: Prior knowledge, beliefs, or experience with STEAM
- The domain of practice: Opportunity to experiment

- The domain of consequence: Perceived student response to the new strategy

The interaction of these processes leads to, or impedes, teacher professional growth (Justi & van Driel, 2006).

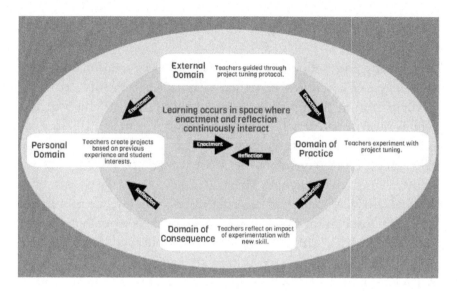

Figure 1
STEAM Teacher Professional Growth Environment
Source: Adapted from Clarke, D., & Hollingsworth, H. (2002). Elaborating a model of teacher professional growth. *Teaching and Teacher Education*, 18(8), 947–967.

Teacher Growth at Panamericano

Embracing this nonlinear and interconnected PD model, we were determined to continue providing the much-needed STEAM PD support to teachers through a model that shifts away from workshop-based PD. Figure 1 illustrates how project tuning was the skill our STEAM coordinators taught all teachers - *the external domain*. Next, teachers were encouraged to incorporate their interests and passions into the STEAM projects they planned - *the personal domain*. Next, the teachers engaged in the project tuning sessions with guidance from STEAM coordinators - *the domain of practice.* Finally, teachers reflected on the effects of the tuning process and its impact on instruction—the domain of consequence. This interconnected process promoted teacher reflection and was an environment deliberately constructed to encourage teacher professional growth.

How Do We Know Teachers Are Growing?

Monitoring and evaluating this process was key to adjusting along the way. We employed three measures: quality of PD, participation in tuning sessions, and the number of high-quality STEAM projects carried out school-wide. After each PD day, we asked teachers to complete an exit survey on the quality and relevancy of the day's activities. We wanted to ensure that the content met the teachers' needs, a key element of effective STEAM PD (Affouneh et al., 2020). Additionally, we monitored teacher participation in tuning sessions, both as a presenter of the project and as a critical colleague. This allowed facilitators to adjust meeting times to minimize impediments to teacher participation. Finally, we tracked the number of STEAM projects that teachers were launching school-wide, which showed an increase of 126%. These indicators suggested that teachers' confidence in their skills was rising.

Lesson 3: Teacher Agency

One of the things that the pandemic did was strip away our sense of agency. As the virus took hold worldwide and authorities started to lock down the population, we felt a loss of control. We no longer had the freedom to leave the house, meet friends, or go to the gym. The same occurred at school. No one asked for virtual learning, yet we were forced to become experts at it suddenly. As schools moved to hybrid and in-person learning, teachers were often left out of decisions on when and how this would occur (Marianno et al., 2022). As we come out of the pandemic, we need to ensure that we return the locus of control to those affected by decisions. We need to give teachers back their agency and involve them as active participants in the decisions that affect them and their students.

What Is Agency?

Bandura (2006) describes agency as an individual's ability to influence one's life circumstances intentionally. A high level of agency means that we have the resources, knowledge, and means to act on our behalf to exert our will. Unfortunately, the pandemic stripped away our ability to act to improve our circumstances. Agency in a school context is when teachers are supported in their ability to affect matters related to their work, decision-making, professional identities, and reform (Tinn & Ümarik, 2021). A concrete way to do this is through distributing leadership by stretching decision-making over various individuals, thus increasing teacher participation in school decisions (Spillane, 2006).

Distributing Leadership in STEAM PD

Since STEAM projects promote active and collaborative principles, our school has deliberately attempted to re-create this in the leadership structure of the PD. The school has two STEAM coordinators, one in charge of the program from kindergarten to grade 5 and the other from grades 6 to 12. They also co-chair a school-wide STEAM committee of experienced STEAM teachers representing each section. This year this committee reviewed the STEAM vision. They conducted surveys and focus groups, gathering feedback to measure how much our vision fit our identity as a school and as STEAM educators. This exercise changed our STEAM vision, broadening its scope and making it more inclusive. This group has also been responsible for identifying gaps in our STEAM PD, leading to modifications in our school calendar to increase PD days and new teacher orientation days dedicated to STEAM PD.

Distributive leadership is correlated with increased teacher efficacy (Abdul Rashid & Abd Latif, 2021). For example, Mancuso et al.'s (2010) study found that a willingness to share decision-making and a distributive leadership style increased teachers' perception of their involvement in school decisions and reduced teacher turnover. Putting structures in place to encourage teachers' voice and participation in decisions that affect them, and their students returns some of the agency that was stripped away during the pandemic and has been shown empirically to improve climate, motivation, and goal achievement (Harris et al., 2007).

Conclusion

School leaders are responsible for promoting the professional learning of all staff. This requires the attention, effort, energy, and time of all involved, often in short supply. Building professional capacity remains a priority, even in a post-pandemic period where teachers' readiness, and their cognitive and emotional energy, may be low. Narrowing the focus of learning to high-leverage skills can facilitate clear expectations and communication, which are critical to promoting teacher readiness to change. Understanding that professional learning will not take a linear progression but will result from teacher experimentation and reflection will promote collaborative practices. Finally, spreading leadership and responsibility among many teachers will ensure that teachers' voices are incorporated in decisions that affect them.

This chapter discusses how we attempt to reconcile the pandemic's demands on teachers with the need to grow as a school in our collective capacity as STEAM educators. It is not a playbook but a snapshot of where we are in our journey. We have and continue to make mistakes. Still, our actions are guided by research, our dedication to ensuring quality learning, and the understanding that the pandemic changed how we approach teacher professional growth. As reflective educators, we need to evolve our approaches to leadership continually and ensure our schools are a great place to work, learn, and teach.

Abdul Rashid, A. R., & Abd Latif, S. (2021). The relationship between distributive leadership and teachers' collective efficacy. *International Journal of Academic Research in Business and Social Sciences*, 11(6). https://doi.org/10.6007/IJARBSS/v11-i6/100

Affouneh, S., Salha, S., Burgos, D., Khlaif, Z., Saifi, A., Mater, N., & Odeh, A. (2020). Factors that foster and deter STEM professional development among teachers. *Science Education*, 104(5), 857–872. https://doi.org/10.1002/sce.21591

Agarwal, N., & Agarwal, R. (2016). Why communities of practice (CoP) are 'still' relevant for the organizations. *Studies in Asian Social Science*, 3(2), 17–25. https://doi.org/10.5430/sass.v3n2p17

Bandura, A. (2006). Toward a psychology of human agency. *Perspectives on Psychological Science*, 1(2), 164–180. https://doi.org/10.1111/j.1745-6916.2006.00011.x

Carter, L. (2017). Neoliberalism and STEM education: Some Australian policy discourse. *Canadian Journal of Science, Mathematics and Technology Education*, 17(4), 247–257. https://doi.org/10.1080/14926156.2017.1380868

Castro Superfine, A., & Li, W. (2014). Developing mathematical knowledge for teaching teachers: A model for the professional development of teacher educators. *Issues in Teacher Education*, 23(1), 113–132.

Clarke, D., & Hollingsworth, H. (2002). Elaborating a model of teacher professional growth. *Teaching and Teacher Education*, 18(8), 947–967.

Dan, Z., & Gary, W. (2018). Teachers' perceptions of professional development in integrated STEM education in primary schools [Conference presentation]. *2018 IEEE Global Engineering Education Conference*, 472–477. https://doi.org/10.1109/EDUCON.2018.8363268

Duhigg, C. (2014). *The Power of Habit*. Random House.

González, S., & Bonal, X. (2021). COVID-19 school closures and cumulative disadvantage: Assessing the learning gap in formal, informal and non-formal education. *European Journal of Education*, 56(4), 607–622. https://doi.org/10.1111/ejed.12476

Guskey, T. R. (2003). What makes professional development effective? *Phi Delta Kappan*, 84(10), 748–750.

Guskey, T. R. (2009). Closing the knowledge gap on effective professional development. *Education Horizons*, 89(4), 224–233.

Harris, A., Leithwood, K., Day, C., Sammons, P., & Hopkins, D. (2007). Distributed leadership and organizational change: Reviewing the evidence. *Journal of Educational Change*, 8(4), 337–347. https://doi.org/10.1007/s10833-007-9048-4

Hilton, A., Hilton, G., Dole, S., & Goos, M. (2015). School leaders as participants in teachers' professional development: The impact on teachers' and school leaders' professional growth. *Australian Journal of Teacher Education*, 40(12), 103–125.

Holt, D., & Vardaman, J. M. (2013). Toward a comprehensive understanding of readiness for change: The case for an expanded conceptualization. *Journal of Change Management*, 13(1), 9–18. https://doi.org/10.1080/14697017.2013.768426

Justi, R., & van Driel, J. (2006). The use of the interconnected model of teacher professional growth for understanding the development of science teachers' knowledge on models and modelling. *Teaching and Teacher Education*, 22(4), 437–450. https://doi.org/10.1016/j.tate.2005.11.011

Keratithamkul, K., Kim, J. N., & Roehrig, G. H. (2020). Cultural competence or deficit-based view? A qualitative approach to understanding middle school students' experience with culturally framed engineering. *International Journal of STEM Education*, 7(26), 1–15. https://doi.org//10.1186/s40594-020-00224-5

Kilpatrick, S., & Fraser, S. (2019). Using the STEM framework collegially for mentoring, peer learning and planning. *Professional Development in Education*, 45(4), 614–626, https://doi.org/10.1080/19415257.2018.1463925

Mancuso, S., Roberts, L., & White, G. (2010). Teacher retention in international schools: The key role of school leadership. *Journal of Research in International Education*, 9(3), 306–323. https://doi.org/10.1177/1475240910388928

Marianno, B. D., Hemphill, A., Loures-Elias, A. P., Garcia, L., Cooper, D., & Coombes, E. (2022). Power in a pandemic: Teachers' unions and their responses to school reopening. *AERA Open*, 8(1), 1–16. https://doi.org/10.1177/23328584221074337

Napier, G., Amborski, D., & Pesek, V. (2017). Preparing for transformational change: A framework for assessing organisational change readiness. *International Journal of Human Resources Development and Management*, 17(1/2), 129. https://doi.org/10.1504/IJHRDM.2017.085265

Rafferty, A. E., Jimmieson, N. L., & Armenakis, A. A. (2013). Change readiness: A multilevel review. *Journal of Management*, 39(1), 110–135. https://doi.org/10.1177/0149206312457417

Spillane, J. P. (2006). *Distributed leadership*. Wiley.

Tinn, M., & Ümarik, M. (2021). Looking through teachers' eyes—investigating teacher agency. *British Journal of Educational Studies*. Advanced online publication. https://doi.org/10.1080/00071005.2021.1960268

Yoon, K. S., Duncan, T., Wen-Yu Lee, S., Scarloss, B. & Shapley, K. L. (2007). Reviewing the evidence on how teacher professional development affects student achievement. *Issues and Answers*, 33, 1–62.

About Dan Yamasaki

Dan Yamasaki is an international educator who works at Colegio Panamericano, where he has been a teacher, principal, and currently, the school director. Before this post, he was an elementary teacher in the Toronto District School Board and a principal at Colegio Granadino in Manizales, Colombia. Dan holds a Master of Arts in Education and is a doctoral candidate at the University of Western Ontario. In addition to this contribution, he wrote a chapter in a teacher resource guide on culturally relevant pedagogy in mathematics and has presented workshops on STEM and project-based learning. Although a passionate educator, he still cannot seem to train his three dogs properly. Dan lives in Bucaramanga, Colombia, with his wife and two sons.

8

Keys to the Kingdom

Curriculum, Instruction, and Assessment

Dr. Spencer Fowler

I sat on the floor with my legs crossed, interacting with a young boy, his younger sister, and their father, in Karak, Jordan. Inside their home, we sat in the living quarters as the mother and elder daughters prepared food and tea in the kitchen. As they entered the room, I stood up to greet them. The bright, sweet platter in their hands kickstarted my furnace amidst the heavy air. I thanked them, and my colleague translated my sentiments. The mother understood me when I mentioned her son's name. At that moment, she bowed her head and buried her face in her hands. When she looked back up, our eyes connected.

I could see the pain she was feeling with him gone, and possibly never able to return. The reality of what we were doing caved my chest in at that moment. Her second-oldest son was at my school, in Beijing, having become the first recipient of the Access Scholarship. The family had fled Syria during the civil war and survived the Zaatari camp. The Access Scholarship provided an opportunity for her son to finish his high school education and chart a new path for him and his family. If we did not place her son, he would be stateless and never able to return to his family. She and her elder daughters then shifted back to the kitchen area. The father, son, and youngest daughter remained with my colleague and me. That was the last time I saw them. I wondered if our recipient, deep in standardized study, inside his dorm over 7000 miles away, would ever see them in his home again.

"The promise is for you and your children and for all who are far off" . . . *With many other words he warned them; and he pleaded with them, "Save yourselves from this corrupt generation."*

– Acts 2:39-40 NIV, The New Testament

The Saint Peter of education, bouncing at the pearly gates of Harvard, NYU, and hundreds of other U.S. mausoleums, has held the position for a century, with no immediate plans to step down. This Saint Peter monopolizes how we judge knowledge, acting as the primary authority on measurement, assessment, evaluation, and promotion. Our patron checks names and results, delivering death strokes to the majority. He gazes out to the cloudy horizon, rejoicing at the lineup of faces from around the world—white, black, brown, and yellow—who readily show him what he loves most: green faces. They will keep coming, in increasing proportion, to see the fate of their future on Judgment Day; though, for all parties concerned, what's the value in a future when every day is *Groundhog Day*?

Standardized testing - as epitomized in the College Board, and as practiced through associated teaching plans, instructional materials, and supplemental tutoring - is destroying education.

It was introduced in the West to assess and filter students and has been used in the East for a couple millennia, particularly in China (Özturgut, 2011); it is ingrained in our education systems and is a focal point for students at almost all levels - from elementary, to high school, and beyond. Standardized testing, the panacea to identify the most capable and worthy, has instead transmogrified our curricula, prioritizing high test scores over learning outcomes, which hurts students and teachers alike. Our overreliance on standardized testing is training people to think in a way that may be useful to ivory tower administrators and

Fortune 500 behemoths who want followers and not leaders; however, it does not help when society has to solve tomorrow's problems using yesterday's solutions. Standardized testing exacerbates existing socioeconomic, gender, and racial differences (Elsesser, 2019), adding to a rat race that leads proponent organizations to one result: dollars. When the status quo prevails, fundamental questions are never asked, and the education industry continues to widen its distance from reality, churning out the same solutions, in the same settings, involving the same types of people - amounting to the single greatest challenge facing education today.

Bind on Earth

A record number of postsecondary institutions embraced a test-optional SAT policy in response to the COVID-19 pandemic (FairTest, 2021). This included the Ivy Leagues, which extended test-optional notices to the class of 2025. This may look like a positive step; it theoretically reduces financial burden and enables more students to secure placement at high-ranking American universities. In practice, from the postsecondary level down, this test-optional policy does not change a thing. Students scrambling to differentiate themselves from their peers will continue to flock to the SATs, and universities will still use test scores while they gladly see their acceptance rates plummet. The debate between mandated versus optional testing obscures the larger problem: the degree to which standardized testing is already integrated with day-to-day education. High scores have supplanted learning outcomes in the educational hierarchy, leading to catastrophe.

Harvard professor Andrew Ho recently doubled down on the value of standardized tests in light of COVID-19, which necessarily impacted student learning (Anderson, 2021). States and school boards, in an effort to understand the degree of impact, have looked to use standardized tests for diagnostic purposes to gage student learning gaps. The relevant question would be: Is society relying on an instrument at a moment when it is most opportune to eschew it? On a more fundamental level: What value does an inadequate measure provide when the results are likely to confirm what is already known (Field, 2021)? Even if there was value in this approach during the pandemic, such use cases for standardized testing are few and far between.

Dating back to the mid-1970s, psychologist Donald T. Campbell was vocal about how society created and measured social policies. He noted that standardized tests may be "useful indicators of school achievement under conditions of normal teaching aimed at general competence" (Campbell, 1976, p. 51). States in America are required to administer standardized tests every year from Grades 3 through 8, and once again in high school; China focuses almost exclusively on test prep and uses standardized testing for college entry. The overarching goal in both cases is to achieve the highest test scores; in service of this goal, school boards in America have linked test results to evaluation, corrupting the very thing it intends to measure.

Campbell critiqued standardized testing by noting "when test scores become the goal of the teaching process, they both lose their value as indicators of educational status and distort the educational process in undesirable ways" (1976, p. 51–52). This position has been forwarded by countless researchers since, indicating that despite society changing radically from the 1970s, little has changed in terms of public policy consequences. Even today, as the pressure to deliver high scores intensifies, so too does the pressure to corrupt those scores; schools distort their teaching practices in an attempt to deliver those high scores, and suddenly a measure meant to understand general competence in select domains becomes education's be-all, end-all focal point.

Schools lying about test results. Parents bribing administrators for high scores. SAT keeping its test the same for a century. Teachers orienting entire curricula toward formulaic test prep.

A few bad apples? No. It is the contemporary education system at work. Test results are used to evaluate students, teachers, and schools. A question like "should our school invest in test prep or educational resources?" loses its ethical dimension when one's livelihood, reputation, and future is staked on test results, making the answer to this question, and others, easier than flipping to the back of the book.

And before this gets political, both Republicans *and* Democrats are responsible for the American predicament. George W. Bush's administration in 2001 introduced No Child Left Behind, which was replaced eight years later by the Obama administration's Race to the Top. Both perpetuated precisely the social science phenomenon discussed by Campbell: They further entrenched standardized testing into school curricula and linked promotion to test results, leading to teachers teaching to the test, school's hiring to the test, and funds being allocated to the test.

As alluded to earlier, there is, of course, a place in school for testing. Quick tests, administered regularly and holding little weight, can improve student retention and deep learning. For its part, standardized testing has value when it is created with specific aims, and when it can guide teachers in adjusting their instructional practices. High-stakes tests are an inferior alternative to a well-rounded education, which - unbeknownst to SAT, ACT, and other purveyors—is not only possible but also beneficial for society. Even today, parents and society in general are struggling to understand: If our kids are not gaining a well-rounded education, and are instead given cookie-cutter tests that do not develop their faculties in a meaningful way, then what are they learning?

Bound in Heaven

A recent report by McKinsey & Company defined the skills and attitudes citizens will need to remain relevant in the workplace of tomorrow (Dondi et al., 2021). Jobs requiring physical skills will decrease, and jobs involving higher cognitive skills will increase. As the report noted, governments must first identify specific skills before they can develop congruent curricula and learning strategies. Citizens will need to add value beyond a machine's capability, feel comfortable in a digital world, and adapt continually to new realities. McKinsey identified four main categories: cognitive, interpersonal, self-leadership, and digital (Dondi et al., 2021). These were subdivided into 13 skills groups, including mental flexibility, developing relationships, entrepreneurship, and understanding digital systems; those groups were then further subdivided into 56 distinct elements of talent (DELTAs). McKinsey ranked the top DELTA proficiencies in terms of employment, high income, and job satisfaction and found that three of the most important proficiencies—coping with uncertainty, synthesizing messages, and self-confidence—happened to have the lowest correlation to education.

It is not surprising, then, that the very first recommendation listed by McKinsey & Company deals with systemic educational reform (Dondi et al., 2021). Beyond reorienting curricula toward the DELTAS and soft skills, the recommendation begins to broach areas seldom considered in policy making circles: What are we teaching our students, and why?

Malcolm Gladwell (2019) explored this by starting with a very simple question: Why do the majority of standardized tests have time constraints? After consulting high-stakes test designers and even chess experts, Gladwell found the time constraints to be arbitrary. He also found standardized testing havens like America value speed over comprehension, underscoring the idea that faster necessarily means better. It is not enough to say that different tasks and jobs require different skill sets; it is that, in any and all situations, the hare is preferable over the tortoise.

This is troubling for a few reasons. In an effort to create fairness and efficiency, society has instead crafted a closed system. Detractors may point out that standardized test scores are an apt predictor of postsecondary grades. As Sternberg (2010, p. 30) noted, that is the point of the tests! If standardized tests are structured in the same manner as final course exams, then it is hardly surprising that, under the same conditions, similar results arise. Society values certain abilities, ability tests are developed to gage said abilities, and the tests are administered to predict performance; then, achievement assessments are created that also evaluate said abilities (Sternberg, 2010, p. 30). The appendages reinforce one another in a system that was built to confirm precisely what is being studied—and nothing else.

It is likewise troubling that society honors foremost those results produced under an archaic, arbitrary system. The standardized testing regime imposes time limits, but who decided on the time limits? Should there be a take-home component instead of a time-limited exam? What do we gain and what do we lose by having constraints on these assessments? Gladwell was concerned with these questions because they allude to our priorities; society's inclination towards speed - instead of depth, creativity, and even accuracy - tell us a great deal about the value society is capturing, and the value society is squandering.

The challenges of tomorrow demand a different approach, predicated on new ways of thinking that bridge communities and leverage capabilities. Society's overreliance on a form of testing may be creating efficient citizens, but is it creating those most capable of leading society through climate change, pandemic, and wealth inequality? It is not that traditional ways are wrong; it is that society went from primarily literate and grew increasingly digital which, according to McLuhan, et al. (1967) began in the early '60s with television's proliferation. Since then, this digital environment has obsolesced older technologies, creating new systems of communicating, organizing, and understanding.

Literate values are important, and we can program environments to amplify positive elements; the problem is that standardized testing, by and large, is a relic from the pre-electric age that does not align with who we are today. New media have moved beyond the strict confines of the compartmentalized standardized testing world, creating new opportunities and new challenges. It follows that a new approach to education would also be necessary.

The guise of certainty is powerful and dangerous. Schools trust an archaic system that provides not truth but merely the semblance of truth. The brass tacks of the student grind, of securing placement in a school and getting a great job, obscure the larger consequences of a system that is training our most talented to think a way counter to the direction society is headed. Tomorrow demands adaptation and fluidity - not stagnation and rigidity. Standardized testing is cementing us to the past.

Watch the Throne

The College Board, as the de facto overseer for SAT- and AP-based assessments, was named as the defendant in a 2019 US District Court class action lawsuit that is ongoing to this day. It is alleged the College Board - which ascertained the names, gender, religious preferences, home addresses, and more from its Student Search Survey - wittingly sold the private information of students to third parties like Facebook, for-profit advertisers, postsecondary institutions, and the military, for as little as $0.42 (Kiesecker, 2019; Masterson, 2019). It is anyone's guess why a registered nonprofit organization - receiving government subsidies and tax-relief in the millions (Phelps, 2018), compensating its CEO more than $1.5 million and staffers $500,000 in 2018 (Kiesecker, 2019), and operating for-profit hedge funds in the Caribbean with a quarter-billion stash (Phelps, 2018) - feels compelled to sell private student information without parental consent, and charge less than a half dollar for it. This is par for the course for the College Board which, over the last decade, has transformed itself into a profit-maximizing firm whose only priority is to leverage its market monopolies and further expand its suite of standardized testing products regardless of their utility.

Rather than acting as one of society's last vestiges for meritocracy, education is increasingly defined by those who are willing to dispense their dollars to gain an advantage. Nothing epitomizes this better than the standardized testing industry, whose gamut of testing fees, preparatory materials, supplemental tutoring, and associated courses contribute to a rat race that cuts across racial and gender lines, compounding disparities rather than diminishing them.

It is not simply that standardized tests tend to favor males over females due to the male propensity to guess, or that whites perform better than blacks which, in itself, is at least partly due to socioeconomic disparities (Perry, 2019). It is that a system has been created that privileges one strata of society over another, and rather than devising ways that would manage these challenges, society seems content to accept the prevailing reality.

Educational challenges stemming from socioeconomic differences will not disappear in the absence of standardized testing; yet it is perplexing that a restrictive, dogmatic system that tilts heavily on the side of the affluent would not encounter vociferous opposition, particularly over the last decade. Consider again the College Board, which has contracts with states and respective school boards to provide K–12 standardized testing. These agreements are in addition to the College Board's full domestic SAT and AP offerings, a pie that expands if we include the international students who pay handsome fees as they clamor for placement. The College Board can record yearly budget surpluses in the hundreds of millions despite it being rife with issues, including recycling tests, awarding seven-figure contracts for nonexistent services rendered, misprinting tests that allocate different time constraints to different groups, developing inferior tests to those used previously, and constructing tests with substantial enough irregularities that they were invalidated (Phelps, 2018). Just as the College Board always gets its cut, so too do the other players in the standardized testing industry - the tutors, prep companies, advertisers, and postsecondary institutions.

It is one thing to prioritize dollars over education; it is another thing for a public-serving nonprofit to abdicate its ethical responsibility and use its hedge funds to bolster its market competitiveness while continuing to solicit taxpayer funding, volunteer support, and donations. This is not a mutually beneficial arrangement; it is a government-sponsored shakedown that leaves society ill-equipped, depleted, and broken.

Family income is one of the primary predictors of postsecondary acceptance, let alone success, and it is easy to see why. Society continues to prop up the standardized education industry despite the lopsided relationship. The College Board's quasi-monopolistic position means it can act with impunity and face little retribution, if any. Its profit-driven behavior is actively endorsed at the state and federal levels, embedding the institution into the bedrock of education. The ancillary standardized testing companies further legitimize this system domestically and internationally, while the advertisers are happy to feed on what is left.

Much of this can disappear tomorrow. Ivy League schools and other American postsecondary institutions can simply amend their requirements and kill standardized testing as we know it. A reversal of this magnitude would lead to a cascade of effects in society down to elementary education, giving us an opportunity to reevaluate our assessment philosophy and develop conscientious curricula for the future. If the rest of the world's postsecondary institutions can eschew it, then why not them? It is not as if world-class research and brain power disappears in the absence of standardized testing.

Universities purportedly value academic freedom. Will they abdicate their responsibility to the public and acquiesce to the industry like the College Board, or will they embrace the spirit of education and challenge orthodoxy? As board members and administrators ponder such a dilemma, it may be worthwhile for them to consider something else more fundamental to education and the industry: If it does not make dollars, does it even make sense to do it?

Conclusion

Standardized testing, the Saint Peter of education, has distorted our curricula, prioritizing test scores instead of learning outcomes, which hurts both students and teachers. Our overreliance on standardized testing is training students to be followers and not leaders, leaving society ill-equipped to solve tomorrow's problems. Standardized testing exacerbates existing socioeconomic, gender, and racial differences, contributing to a rat race that leads proponent organizations to financial windfalls at the expense of society. Absent corrective action, the education industry will continue to widen its distance from reality, offering the same solutions, in the same settings, involving the same people. Standardized education, as manifested in standardized testing, represents the greatest challenge facing education today.

As Saint Peter's reign continues, the school boards, teachers, students, and parents will persistently pour money into the industry's bottomless pit. If we value our children and their future, it is incumbent on us to press ahead and question the viability of a broken system. We can break the cycle of docility and equip ourselves with the tools to rise up against tomorrow's challenges.

Anderson, J. (2021). Harvard edcast: Student testing, accountability, and COVID. *Harvard Graduate School of Education*. March 11, 2021. https://www.gse.harvard.edu/news/21/03/harvard-edcast-student-testing-accountability-and-covid

Campbell, D. T. (1976). *Assessing the impact of planned social change*. Occasional Paper #8, pp. 51–52. Public Affairs Center, Dartmouth College.

Dondi, M., Klier, J., Panier, F., & Schubert, J. (2021, June 25). *Defining the skills citizens will need in the future world of work*. McKinsey & Company. https://www.mckinsey.com/industries/public-and-social-sector/our-insights/defining-the-skills-citizens-will-need-in-the-future-world-of-work

Elsesser, K. (2019, December 11). Lawsuit claims SAT and ACT are biased - here's what research says. *Forbes*. https://www.forbes.com/sites/kimelsesser/2019/12/11/lawsuit-claims-sat-and-act-are-biased-heres-what-research-says/?sh=197eca563c42

FairTest. (2021, December 1). Test-optional growth chronology 2005–2021f. https://www.fairtest.org/sites/default/files/Optional-Growth-Chronology.pdf

Field, K. (2021, February 12). To test or not to test? Educators weigh the value of standardized testing during pandemic. *The Hechinger Report*. https://hechingerreport.org/to-test-or-not-to-test-educators-weigh-the-value-of-standardized-testing-during-a-pandemic/

Gladwell, M. (2019, June 20). Puzzle rush [Audio podcast]. *In Revisionist history*. https://www.pushkin.fm/show/revisionist-history/

Kiesecker, C. (2019, July 21). Parents question College Board's use of student data. *Parent Coalition For Student Privacy*. https://studentprivacymatters.org/parents-question-college-boards-use-of-student-data/

Masterson, M. (2019, December 10). New lawsuit claims College Board illegally sold student data. *WTTW News*. https://news.wttw.com/2019/12/10/new-lawsuit-claims-college-board-illegally-sold-student-data

McLuhan, M., et al. (1967). The Medium Is the Massage. Berkeley: Gingko Press.

Özturgut, O. (2011). Standardized testing in the case of China and the lessons to be learned for the U.S. *Journal of International Education Research*, 7(2), 1–6.

Perry, A. M. (2019, May 17). Students need more than an SAT adversity score, they need a boost in wealth. *Brookings*. https://www.brookings.edu/blog/the-avenue/2019/05/17/students-need-more-than-an-sat-adversity-score-they-need-a-boost-in-wealth/

Phelps, Richard. (2018). Does College Board deserve public subsidies? *Nonpartisan Education Review.* https://nonpartisaneducation.org/Review/Articles/v14n7.htm

Sternberg, Robert J. (2010). *College admissions for the 21st century.* Harvard University Press.

About Dr. Spencer Fowler

Dr. Spencer A. Fowler is the CEO and Superintendent of the Affiliated High School of Peking University's Dalton Academy. He has spent nearly two decades educating students and building programs in Chile, China, Egypt, Germany, South Africa, Spain, Thailand, and Vietnam. Dr. Fowler is breaking the rigid mold of standardized education and replacing it with bespoke, student-centric curricula. His innovative ideas have attracted the attention of Harvard University and the Colombian Ministry of Education.

Dr. Fowler initiated China's first access scholarship, enabling high school students from war-torn regions to complete their education at China's foremost academic institution. He spearheaded an eight-figure fundraising campaign, coordinated campus expansion in Beijing, and opened a satellite campus 2,283km away in Haikou. Dr. Fowler is intent on spreading his educational philosophy beyond China.

Dr. Fowler holds a BA and BEd from Queen's University, an MEd from the College of New Jersey, and an EdD from Western University. He is a member of the Ontario College of Teachers and has received a Principal Certification, Educational Leadership Certificate, and a Manitoba Teacher Certification. Dr. Fowler's publications include his 2019 dissertation *Chinese Public Education and Global Social Justice: The Organizational Challenges of Initiating an Access Scholarship in a Chinese Public School,* and book chapter "Chinese Public Education and Social Justice" in Griffiths, Lowrey, and Cassar's *The Leader Reader: Narratives of Experiences.*

9

Real Learning: My Educational Journey to Purpose

Curriculum, Instruction, and Assessment

Robert Rinaldo

"Education is not preparation for life, education is life itself."

–John Dewey (October 20, 1859–June 1, 1952), American philosopher and educator

My career in education has been a continuous learning experience in leadership, confidence, and self-awareness. My journey in this field spans several continents, where I have gone from a teacher in rural upstate New York, a principal in Tegucigalpa, Honduras, and a head of school in Costa Rica and now Abu Dhabi. Every step of the way, I have wanted to be part of something excellent, but excellence is not always guaranteed. As I reflect on my career, I have realized that some of my greatest leadership lessons came from failure. Learning from failure started me on a path to discovering my why, my purpose in the education. Understanding my why has unlocked my ability to navigate change and led me to an unwavering belief in students and their potential. It just so happens that my why is also my life purpose and what I believe to be the most important aspiration for any leader: to help develop confidence in others so that they may strive in good times and, most importantly, grow through adversity.

Teach, Fail, Grow

My first real job was making my way through the classroom as a high school social studies teacher in the Catskills region of upstate New York. I say "making my way through" because as a recent college graduate teaching high school history, I struggled. My curriculum was very textbook oriented, and my instructional methodology was to stay one day ahead of students in the assigned readings and then deliver notes on the material as if I was an expert on the subject. I was the sage on the stage.

My main teaching objective that first year was to maintain control. I expected students to behave, diligently copy notes, and then memorize those notes to regurgitate on a test. The assessment would usually, in some way or another, ask students to show their understanding of events and interpretations of those events. Comparing and contrasting, finding the main idea, developing a chronological historical focus, citizenship issues, and proper behavior were important skills. However, it was not at all important if the information or content was retained. Even if the information was retained, it was just information. What students did with their information was hard to discern, and frankly it did not matter to me if I did my job to transmit my knowledge to students and they could demonstrate that they passively absorbed the material.

By high school, most students were familiar with the routines and were capable of following directions. I was training students for the world of work, as an employee, instilling employability skills. I expected punctuality and strict adherence to my classroom rules and regulations. If you needed to state your thoughts, concerns, or opinions, there was a procedure to follow. Assessments were very subjective and could be measured through multiple-choice quizzes and tests, matching, or fill-in-the-blank exercises. I created a competitive environment where you were rewarded on your ability to absorb content and show a level of skills

90

proficiency, and then ranked in a hierarchy based on your ability to memorize and restate the information at a specified time. I dissuaded any attempt at risk taking, and mistakes or failures were held against you and then averaged into your grade at the end of a unit, semester, or academic year. It was an environment that had very little to do with creativity or original thought, in return for compliance, amenability, and obedience.

Most of the students played the game very well. They competitively worked hard to get the best grade possible, complying with the teachers' requests and padding their averages for a future college application process. The final product or grade was all that mattered in lieu of a collaborative learning process that had fundamental meaning to the student and their life. For every three or four students who took the class seriously and saw it as a vehicle to a prosperous future, there was another that intrinsically could not understand the purpose of formal education and unknowingly saw through the nonauthentic charade by reacting in one of three different ways:

1. *Going through the motions*

One subset of students would simply attend class without showing much interest or desire to participate, choosing to take limited notes and take a risk on the hope or chance that at test time that they had a rudimentary understanding of the content. They were the students who did just enough to get by without failing or receiving a below-average grade, pleasing their parents and teachers to an acceptable extent. Acceptable in that the prevalent rationale was that not all could be "A" students or high achievers (although some were). Some had to be on the ascending side of the bell curve.

2. *Needing extra support*

The second type were the students who also wanted to please and comply but did not have the ability to achieve success as defined. These students maybe did not have the gift to memorize well, or possessed a learning need such as dyslexia, or a social-emotional, sensory, or physical need. Usually, these students would receive extra support in the form of further explanation, added time, or homework, quiz, and test modifications. In many instances over the course of my career, these were the students who were encouraged to just turn in the work and behave. By doing so they received a completion grade and along with good behavior got a passing grade. Acquiring useful life skills or showing their ability to use their skills and their learning to make an impact, or discover an interest, was never considered as a requisite for these students.

3. Rebelling with a cause

The final student type was the student who not only saw through the charade but was going to find a way to shine and show his skills by rebelling against the system and gaining attention and a name by disrupting. For me, a first-year teacher who believed success meant having obedient students who submitted to my belief of what education should be, that student type was personified by Jimmy B.

Jimmy taught me a valuable lesson during my initial year as a classroom teacher that would take me years to fully understand. Jimmy was a charismatic 16-year-old, full of energy. He was well-liked by fellow classmates because he was caring and the first to come to your aid if you needed help. Jimmy did not want to be controlled, and for a 22-year-old first-year teacher whose main objective was to have control, there was friction and discipline. Discipline, as I look back on it now, that I am not proud of. There was no dignity in the way I insisted Jimmy follow my rules. On occasions I engaged in back-and-forth arguments with Jimmy in front of the class, showing I was not ready to lead students. My *why* as an educator was still being developed and in the wake of my process was Jimmy B.

The sad part of this example is the potential damage done to the psyche and confidence of so many students. I believe that it was possible that the students in the three categories mentioned above did not know that they were being stifled from showing their intelligence, creativity, and innate desire to learn, due to the curriculum, instructional methodologies, and the asserted purpose of formal education of the time. Many thought they were of lesser intelligence or ability. There can be nothing more damaging than systematically and needlessly adding fear, doubt, and uncertainty to a young person's life without knowing the potential long-term effects of our practice.

As head of school, I have often said to colleagues, teachers, and students that we all have the responsibility to lead and model the behaviors and beliefs of our community. If leadership requires appreciation, trust, and forming a bond, then I failed Jimmy. It was not so much that I stifled his creativity, it was that I did not connect and understand his desires, aspirations, and fears.

My experience that year had been challenging but there were also many rewards and opportunities for personal and professional growth. I did motivate students to "achieve" in the classroom, and I want to believe that I provided support and hope to some. I worked with students outside the classroom in athletics, and above all I gained valuable professional work experience as a member of a school faculty. And when I ran off the road on a snowy and blustery winter night, Jimmy B. was there with his dad's tow truck to get me out of the snow drift.

Getting to Your Why

Knowing that working in education would be my ultimate career goal, but still in a process of self-awareness, I left the formal setting to begin an international volunteer grassroots

93

development experience with the United States Peace Corps. It was during the intensive five-month Peace Corps training program, which was integral to your success as a volunteer, with a cross-cultural, technical, and language acquisition focus, that I realized certain commonalities existed in all learning. These commonalities would serve as the foundation of my teaching principles on my eventual return to the classroom. They included an interest in the topic, an emotional connection to the activity, a motivating challenge, a self-paced experience with trial and error, a desire to achieve mastery, and inspiring teachers and trainers.

Along with twelve other aspiring volunteers in the cohort, we worked hard each day preparing for our eventual move from training to a two-year commitment of service in a rural Central American community. In terms of learning, my Peace Corps experience served as the most effective model of education or schooling that I received. I applied previously learned skills and knowledge with intensive Spanish-language, cross-cultural, and technical training to assist in the planning and implementation of small animal husbandry projects. From that experience, I learned more of the socioeconomic and cultural realities of the world and developed an awareness, consciousness, and empathy that I was not able to develop in more traditional educational settings. My Peace Corps experience was truly authentic and meaningful, and ultimately helped define my life's purpose as an international educator. It was here that I used what I learned and applied my skills and knowledge in real-world situations with the purpose of impacting communities and adding value. This meaningful teaching and learning experience confirmed my belief in the value of student-centered instruction and relationships and a commitment to purpose.

After completion of my service and return to the field of education, I began to apply and modify lessons learned. Year after year in the classroom, and then as a principal, and later as a head of school, I shared my learning and developed an appreciation and joy in my day-to-day interactions with all students. Again, the example of Jimmy was noteworthy in my development. He expressed his needs through acting out against the structure of the class. Yet how many others remained silent? As a teacher and then a principal, I would make an intentional effort to identify and reach out to all students and teachers. Sunday evenings would become a time of reflection on those I had not connected with during the week. I came to see that successful school leadership stemmed from an intrinsic desire to see students succeed and grow as confident individuals. Reflecting on my career, I know now that any success I may have experienced can be attributed to the fact that I have only been able to see the good and potential in all my students. I genuinely believed in students even when they themselves were unsure or doubting. For many years without having articulated my own purpose, I now find and am convinced that my career as a school leader, and the role of any current or aspiring teacher, principal, or head of school, is to help students find their confidence in all aspects of their lives and become the assertive leaders that they are born to be. I found that a simple word of encouragement or a comment expressing interest in an aspect of the student's life, if genuine, can have an enormous impact and lead to conviction and self-assurance. I have attempted to empower students to assume leadership roles and always said yes to an idea or potential activity that would lend to student agency, allowing an opportunity to take a risk in the planning and implementation of any activity that could potentially add value to the greater school or local community.

There is an urgency for school leaders to become intentional in defining what it means to be student centered in instruction and in relationships. Today we hear of the need to transform education, and for all the talk and attempts at innovative practices, many international school classrooms are still as traditional and teacher centered in their approach and methods as was the case from my initial teaching experience. The opportunity to add value or propose a solution to a problem, and then to receive feedback and be recognized for your work, creates an excitement on campus similar to a sports tournament, concert, play, or student-sponsored activity. Once the learning becomes authentic and purposeful, a momentum is created that cannot be stopped. In a work published by the United Nations Organization for Economic Co-operation and Development (OECD; 2018), *The Future of Education and Skills: Education 2030*, it was noted that future-ready students need to exercise agency: "Agency implies a sense of responsibility to participate in the world and, in so doing, to influence people, events and circumstances for the better. Agency requires the ability to frame a guiding purpose and identify actions to achieve a goal" (OECD, 2018, p. 4).

Embracing Change

Transformation or a revolution in teaching and learning will come, and if not led by new technologies, national or local policy reform, and curriculum design, it will be led by school communities that believe the fundamental purpose of education is to add value. As a school leader, I have had the great fortune to contribute to and witness numerous meaningful projects that had a profound impact on communities, carried out by students without adult prompting. One that comes to mind was an initiative of two former high school students at the Lincoln School in Costa Rica. They identified a problem and were concerned with the number of leftover meals from the school cafeteria that were thrown away each day, instead of being donated to the hungry or needy. On a larger scale throughout the country, they found that due to liability issues it was against the law to donate perishable leftover food. Their solution was a bill proposed to the Costa Rican Congress that created a feasible way for benefactors in Costa Rica to donate perishable foods. It was aimed at freeing benefactors from the legal issues involved in donating so long as they adhered to certain safety standards.

These students were motivated by a goal of reducing hunger and used their skills to take action.

This project (and others that included entrepreneurial efforts characterized by the creation of socially responsible business concepts; campaigns designed to promote the benefits of and need for agrobiodiversity and sustainability; beautifully produced student chamber concerts and student photographic exhibits and auctions to raise awareness and lend support to diverse social and medical associations; student produced, directed, and performed musical stage productions; and projects that incorporated the arts to motivate the principles of discipline, determination, and perseverance in children of local marginalized communities) was all completely student led and made a substantial impact on their communities. They are a testament to the type of student outcomes that need to be valued and supported.

However, even though these initiatives and accomplishments created an increased sense of community pride, many were not developed within the objectives and goals of the written curriculum. It is curious to consider that these important student initiatives were created, planned, and implemented by students on their own, to demonstrate what mattered to them in their lives and how they could use their learning to make a difference. Parallel to these experiences, and at the same time, students were still being held responsible in the classroom to fulfill the requirements of a fragmented course load. Real life and more authentic learning appeared to be happening outside the classroom, and for me, this has served as the most resounding and clear argument of today's learners taking matters into their own hands and asking for purpose.

Interconnected with student-centered instruction is student wellness. When we offer students opportunities to identify problems and a methodology to find solutions, we increase the possibilities for creativity, curiosity, empathy, and compassion.

This ultimately leads to increased confidence and contributes to wellness. A 2019 study published in the *Journal of Clinical Psychiatry* found the presence of meaning in life is associated with better physical and mental well-being (Aftab et al., 2019). As an educational leader, instruction that encourages the search for and presence of meaning is the main factor in student wellness.

Leading change starts with a belief that all decisions made must be in the best interest of students. Community buy-in starts by celebrating and encouraging student initiatives and projects and using the momentum generated on campus to create a shared excitement and appreciation of the impact of student learning. I am reminded of a former Lincoln high school student leader, Nicole, that pitched an idea at the 2016 Diamond Challenge. The Diamond Challenge is the leading high school entrepreneurial contest in the world. With thousands of ideas pitched each year, Nicole's project was a social business that created healthy soda from exotic Costa Rican fruits and supported community development by buying from local farmers. Her success as a 2016 Diamond Challenge finalist was celebrated throughout the school community and as a result students began searching avenues to pitch their ideas. The MIT Launch, connection with the Harvard Innovation Lab, hosting regional Diamond Challenge events all sparked interest and student enthusiasm. By witnessing the impact of student projects that were adding social value outside of the stated curriculum, a community effort led by a shared vision from a committed and talented board of directors, school leadership, teachers, parents, and students, was made. Again, with school community support, a relationship was developed with Babson College to implement an entrepreneurial methodology that anchored student projects to the United Nations Sustainable Development Goals. Transferring this momentum into a community wide vision for teaching and learning and basing all decisions from hiring to facilities design and learning spaces, to capital expenditures, to aligned professional development, to supportive curriculum and assessment policies, to class electives and choice were made with a shared definition of student-centered instruction and relationships in mind.

It takes a community effort and belief to lead the change, and as a community, if we agree with Dewey that, "The educational end and ultimate test of the value of what is learned is its use and application in carrying on and improving the life of all," (1934, p. 202), then the question that needs to be put forward is when.

Aftab, A., Lee, E. E., Klaus, F., Daly, R., Wu, T.-C., Tu, X., Huege, S., & Jeste, D. V. (2019). Meaning in life and its relationship with physical, mental, and cognitive functioning: a study of 1,042 community-dwelling adults across the lifespan. *Journal of Clinical Psychiatry*, 80(1), 19m13064. https://doi.org/10.4088/JCP.19m13064

Dewey, J. & Hinchey, P. H. (2019). *Moral Principles in Education and My Pedagogic Creed by John Dewey : With a Critical Introduction by Patricia H. Hinchey*. Myers Education Press.

Dewey, J. (2010). The need for a philosophy of education (1934). *The University of Chicago Press Journals*, 7(2), p. 202.

OECD. (2018). The future of education and skills: Education 2030. *The Future We Want*, pp. 1–21. https://www.oecd.org/education/2030-project/contact/E2030%20Position%20Paper%20(05.04.2018).pdf

About Robert Rinaldo

Robert Rinaldo is currently head of school at the GEMS American Academy, Abu Dhabi. Robert has extensive international experience in both formal and informal educational settings, as a US Peace Corps volunteer, teacher, athletic director, principal, and head of school. His accomplishments include the implementation of transformational student-centered learning experiences that encourage an entrepreneurial mindset, where students use their learning to make a positive impact on society. His student-centered philosophy stresses a holistic approach with purposeful and authentic student academic, artistic, athletic, and service-learning opportunities. In addition to school leadership roles, Robert has served as an independent school board consultant advising on the strategic planning process, accreditation, and school improvement planning. He has also held the position of president of the Association of Bi-lingual Schools of Honduras (ABSH) and served on the board of the Association of American Schools of Central America (AASCA). Robert holds degrees in teaching and educational leadership from the State University of New York and Nova Southeastern University and is a Columbia University Klingenstein Fellow.

10

Strategic Planning? Well, It Ain't About Strategies!

School Improvement

Dr. Bill Johnston

Several years ago, I was asked by a colleague to facilitate some board consulting work to help with their strategic planning process. After discussing the work I did with a results-based structure I had been developing, we confirmed the direction and mapped out a schedule and agenda.

We spent the first day working on the basics: mission, vision, values, and strategic goals based on the five areas given in my model. The board expected to begin an environmental scan and develop strategies to meet the goals we set. They were surprised when I reminded them that we needed to outline accountability structures by developing more detailed definitions and measures before going to environmental scanning and strategies. After a short discussion, however, they were clearer on what had been given to them earlier and were excited about the concept.

The work began. As we got into more detail, I noticed looks of growing concern on the faces of about half the board members, and some blank stares from the others. I called a break to informally gather their concerns. Before I could start opening the questions, the board members took their coffee and began a side conversation. The school head and I sipped our coffee, and waited.

That side meeting broke off and folks returned for more coffee and then sat down to get back to work. As I put down my coffee, the board president said, "Dr. Johnston, I am afraid that we all agree that as a board, we are not ready for this yet. We like the concept and want to do it, but we just don't know enough to be able to go ahead right now. Can we use the rest of the time to firm up our foundations and then to learn more about how to go about this?"

So, we did.

LEADERSHIP LESSON: *Strategic planning must focus on student growth and development. A focus on student growth and development is woven throughout the plan, starting with foundational documents, and moving all the way through performance accountability structures and the development of activities to reach outcome targets.*

Strategic planning in international schools has been around a long time—my first contact with it as a head of school was at a 1989 conference presentation by Dr. Bill Cook. Dr. Cook's big idea was that strategic planning had to hinge on accountability and that "the success of any plan is determined only by the results if produces" (Cook, 1988, p. 94). Unfortunately, many organizations have come to focus more on completing plan activities and have lost sight of where the focus should be: student growth and development (Johnston, 2012a).

There are any number of approaches to strategic planning (Bryson, 2011). We will take a walk through a process designed to ensure that focus remains central to the entire planning enterprise, from philosophical foundations all the way to plan execution.

1. Who Is Involved?

The governing body or board is responsible for building a strategic plan, and it will have to give formal approval to anything developed by a facilitated planning team. The most effective efforts involve a planning committee comprised of two or three members of the board and one or two members from each of the school's core constituencies (e.g., administration, instructional staff, parents, and students). Look for balance—you will want a representative committee, but you don't want the group so large it becomes unwieldy. The ideal size for a work team appears to be five or six (Harrison, 2021; Scholtes et al., 1996), but I recommend going as high as eight or nine to gain more diverse representation and (hopefully) broader political support. This will make the facilitator's job more of a challenge but, in my experience, it is well worth the effort. You can also help meet that challenge by requiring all members to report back to the groups they were picked to represent at specific points in the process by offering general feedback opportunities as a part of the process and expanding involvement. You will want to keep that in mind as we go through the process.

2. Build a Foundation

Foundational documents are well named: they establish the big-picture basis for everything that will come. It is best to begin with a statement of educational philosophy or core beliefs. You can facilitate the process by starting with a general discussion of what, as a school, you believe about education. I like to begin with a short opening discussion about the task itself, then give the group twenty to thirty belief statements gleaned from other schools around the world to discuss, add to, delete, or otherwise edit to get to a list of no more than ten statements that reflect what they see as the school's educational beliefs. That is the beginning.

Taking the Statement of Educational Beliefs as a starting point, the committee would then move to develop a list of the school's Core Values. I like to define them as those qualities of the human condition that the school values the most. As with the Statement of Educational Beliefs, the process is facilitated by starting with a large pool of materials generated by previous online research into what other schools have done. Once that list has been generated, it is critical that the committee specifically address a question that will come up again and again: Does the list of Core Values align tightly with our Statement of Educational Beliefs? If that connection cannot be clearly shown by putting them side by side, then the committee will have to make some changes to one or the other, or both, until they do clearly align. Once final drafts are ready, they should go to the board for its review, discussion, and adoption. No further work should be done until the board acts.

With Beliefs and Values in hand, the committee can then move to develop a Mission Statement. Anyone who has been in any formal organization has had extensive contact with mission statements. Just as a reminder, the mission statement describes who/what the school is and the needs it exists to fulfill—it's a statement of "*why* it should be doing what it does" (Bryson, 2011, p. 127). The school will likely already have one and, assuming so, the first task is to revisit the central question: Does the mission statement align tightly with our Statement of Educational Beliefs and our Core Values? If it does not, or if the committee feels that the mission does not clearly state the school's raison d'être, then it will need to be revised or rewritten. Again, the use of extensive examples from other places can be very helpful in that process.

The final foundational document takes our first step toward accountability. The Vision Statement is a short narrative description of what the school would look like upon realization of its mission: it is an outcome statement. The Vision, however, is a general description and—at this level, at least—is not geared to including specific measures (Bryson, 2011; National

Association of Independent Schools [NAIS], 2007). Those will come later.

As an example, here is the Vision Statement used by an international school:

> [The International School] is recognized as the premier English-language early childhood through secondary school in [Host Country]. The internationally recognized program is actively sought out by all National and International parents who truly want to join a partnership to provide the very best education possible for their children. Students at [the International School] are young people of high integrity from diverse backgrounds, working together in a friendly, respectful, positive environment. They achieve at high levels within the school's challenging curriculum. This curriculum emphasizes strong academics, inquiry-based learning, multiculturalism, and application of critical thinking skills. Athletic teams compete successfully both at home and abroad. Student work in the graphic and performing arts regularly draws high accolades, demonstrating high levels of competence and representing a wide range of cultural perspectives. Students demonstrate a strong social consciousness and are actively involved in projects promoting local and global stewardship. Graduates attend the institutions of higher learning of their choice, and become responsible economic, social, and political leaders not only in [our home country], but also across our increasingly interdependent world.

There are some very specific targets voiced in this vision and, while there are allusions to performance indicators, no measures or performance levels are specified. This vision is almost exclusively about students and says nothing about how to achieve the targets: it just verbalizes them clearly and succinctly. Not only is it functional, but this is also one heck of an inspirational statement! The Vision Statement compiled, it must then pass the consistency test: Does it align with the Beliefs, Core Values, and Mission Statement already adopted by the board? If so, it, too, would go to the board for its formal adoption.

Foundational documents, once adopted by the board, should be reviewed at least every five years to be sure that the nature of the school has not changed (Bryson, 2011; McCune, 1987; NAIS, 2007). Ideally, they would last at least ten years without major change.

3. Identify Outcome Areas

We have remained at a general level thus far, building a firm foundation of consistent and connected statements of educational beliefs, core values, mission, and vision. Having gone from nothing to establishing the foundation, we need to start to get more specific to tighten up understanding of the direction the school will take to realize its vision. I support using the SAAGE model to address this need (Johnston, 2012a).

SAAGE is an acronym that speaks to five outcome areas: Scholarship (or student achievement), Athletics, the Arts, Global citizenship, and Enrollment. The first four address the prime areas of student development. The last, Enrollment, addresses the critical resource that drives all efforts in a tuition-supported international school.

The outcome statements developed for each of these areas should be worded as very broad outcomes. They are very simple, almost just place holders, and are the boundaries for establishment of performance indicators and targeted performance outcomes. As an example, the outcome for Scholarship could be as simple as "Students will perform at high academic levels." The statement is, essentially, a group label.

4. Define Performance Metrics: SMART Goals

SMART goals came on the educational scene some fifteen years ago, developed with classroom use in mind (Conzimious & O'Neill, 2006). The structure also works very well when defining what the outcome areas mean. Put another way, we will be coming up with school performance targets that are Specific, Measurable, Attainable, Realistic, and Time constrained to be able to paint a picture of what we want out of each area.

"Paint a picture" is a very important phrase. The idea here is to create a set of performance indicators that will be used as a group to determine if the school is making progress toward achieving the stated outcome. Given the requirement for connection and consistency, that would also mean progress toward realizing the vision by fulfilling the mission through application of the educational beliefs and core values.

It is also important to remember that, by definition, the time constraint means the goal must be met within five years of its establishment and the performance level would be expected to be maintained.

Because we will be looking at performance on the SMART goals as a group, we need to be sure there are enough of them in a given outcome area to define the area adequately, but not so many that it becomes unwieldy. I suggest developing a minimum of three and no more than ten for each outcome area, recalling that each SMART goal must reflect the foundational documents. Again, examples may be the best way to understand this concept. Here is a short list of academic SMART goals.

- Ninety percent of students will show one year of growth on the school's adopted standardized tests in reading and mathematics.
- Eighty percent of seniors will take three or more International Baccalaureate (IB) examinations.
- Ninety percent of IB examinations taken by school seniors will earn a score of four (4) or higher.

Each goal is very specific, identifies a measure and performance level, is attainable (given the nature of the clientele that normally attends international schools), and is realistic. Each speaks to high academic performance and is student centered. Each is an outcome - a result set that defines the area in terms of accountability.

5. Environmental Scan

Environmental scanning is simply taking a detailed look at the organization and the community. In other words, it is about understanding the context in which the school functions (Waechter, 2010). Scanning is commonly referred to as a SWOT Analysis: a review of organizational *S*trengths, *W*eaknesses, *O*pportunities, and *T*hreats. Strengths and weaknesses refer to things *inside* the organization (for example, student performance, attendance, enrollment data; teacher qualifications and turnover; condition of facilities, levels of community involvement). Opportunities and threats look to things *outside* the organization (for example, government regulation, relationship with local authorities, economic development and conditions, political issues, outside community perceptions of the school). Scanning would necessarily include generating the baseline data on all SMART goals developed earlier, and each goal should be reexamined in light of those data to be sure that the goal is considered *R*easonable and *A*ttainable within the five-year *T*ime constraint. Finally, they must all be adopted by the board.

6. Establish an Accountability Schedule

The board or governing body is responsible for monitoring progress toward reaching adopted outcomes, as defined by the SMART goals in each area. Data should be presented annually, and the board should draw a conclusion to determine if satisfactory progress is being made. This aspect can make many people nervous, but the intended process, Preponderance of Evidence (CAEP), has been used for years in school accreditation, despite some shifts to fully quantify this qualitative process of formal professional review (Johnston, 2012; Worthen & Sanders, 1976). In brief, the board would look at all the data for a given outcome area and make a consensus decision on whether progress is being made toward reaching the *outcome*. Commentary on individual data points is, of course, to be welcomed, but the accountability question is done on the overall performance.

7. Develop Strategies to Reach Targets

Here we are - *strategies* for a strategic plan! You will remember that the plan until now has focused entirely on students and what *they* should be able to do: they really are the reason for schools to exist. Strategies shift focus to the adults in the organization. Strategies define what adults will do to facilitate students reaching the first four SAAGE outcomes (i.e., Scholarship, Athletics, the Arts, and Global citizenship). They come from information gleaned from brainstorming (Scholtes et al., 1996), the SWOT analysis, and other research. The core question is how to facilitate student development in each of the goal areas, often across goal areas. Once done, of course, the board must adopt them and, when it comes to put those strategies into effect, the board will also need to provide funding through the budget process.

Again, some examples may help clarify those connections.

Scholarship: The data show that student achievement is not what the school wants. A closer look shows that while the school has a strong staff, half of it is internationally hired and the average stay is less than three years. It looks like something must be done to stabilize staffing to enhance continuity and performance. Adults must do something there - whatever is developed to address it will be a strategy developed with Scholarship in mind, but which will also impact Athletics, the Arts, and Global Citizenship.

Athletics: The data show that a small group of students participate in athletics and that team performance in games and tournaments is weak. Discussions with coaches, students, parents, and others raise questions about perceived school commitment, adequacy of facilities, scheduling conflicts with other areas, among other issues. Adopted strategies went across facilities planning, staffing recruitment and retention, and administrative and departmental communication.

8. In Closing . . .

This has been a very quick overview of a rather involved topic, but I hope that it has opened topics for thought and discussion. That said, I will leave you with some summary points:

1. Strategic Planning is *not* about the strategies: it is about documenting who you are as a school - what you believe and value, your purpose, and your vision of the future for your students.
2. Strategic Planning is a process used to clarify expectations for what students should be able to do and for who you would want them to become... defining each of those concepts operationally.
3. Strategic Planning is about understanding context and finding ways to facilitate the student growth and development you, as a school, exist to realize.

4. Strategic Planning is about accountability for *student* results, not about adults completing the strategies.

Bryson, J. M. (2011). *Strategic planning for public and non-profit organizations.* Jossey-Bass.

CAEP (Council for the Accreditation of Educator Preparation). (n.d.). Glossary. caepnet.org/glossary?letter=P,

Conzimious, A., & O'Neill, J. (2006). *The power of SMART Goals: Using goals to improve student learning.* Solution Tree Press.

Cook, W. J. (1988). *Bill Cook's strategic planning for America's schools.* Association of American School Administrators.

Harrison, K. (2020, June 1). *What's the ideal number of people in a work team or committee?* https://cuttingedgepr.com/whats-ideal-number-people-work-team-committee/

Johnston, W. F. (2012a). A data framework to support strategic planning. In B. Bendrick & D. Willows (Eds.), *Effective data management for schools* (pp. 68–71). John Catt Educational.

Johnston, W. F. (2012b). *Ready, fire, aim: Is AdvancED shooting itself in the foot?* InterEd, Fall 2012.

McCune, S. D. (1986). *Guide to strategic planning for educators.* ASCD.

National Association of Independent Schools (NAIS). (2007). *The strategic process: 10 steps for planning your independent school's future.* NAIS.

Scholtes, P. R., Joiner, B. L, & Streibel, B. J. (1996). *The TEAM handbook* (2nd ed.). Oriel.

Waechter, S. A. (2010). *Driving strategic planning: A non-profit executive's guide* (2nd ed). BoardSource.

Worthen, B. R. & Sanders, J.R., (1976). *Educational evaluation: alternative approaches and practical guidelines.* Longman.

About Dr. Bill Johnston

Bill Johnston holds a BA from Dickinson College and M.Ed. and Ed.D degrees from Virginia Tech. His 45-year career includes teaching intermediate, middle, high school and graduate school students as well as over 35 years of experience as a school administrator, 25 of them as Head of School in international schools in Brazil, Uruguay, Kuwait and Ecuador. He has also served as an in-house expert or external consultant on governance and administrative issues to Boards, School Administrations and Organizations in the US, Brazil, Ecuador, Colombia, and Venezuela. He has served as editor of six books and has authored 15 articles in professional journals and six program evaluation research studies. He has also made over 50 conference presentations in English, Spanish and Portuguese, and his contributions to the profession have been recognized through awards presented by the Virginia Educational Research Association, the Virginia Council on Learning Disabilities, the Virginia Educational Technology Advisory Committee, the Ecuadorian Ministry of Education, and the Association of American Schools in Latin America (AASSA). Bill retired in 2016 and loves spending the extra time with his wife, three children and their spouses, and five grandchildren.

11

A Successful Change Agent Leads with Integrity

School Improvement

Dr. Colin Brown

The change agent - sounds glamorous, right? Let me assure you, it is not. I suppose the role could be likened to that of a bull rider. Everything is calm beforehand; the audience, the bull rider's team, and investors are all waiting with eager anticipation—will the rider be successful? The gate swings open and suddenly the bull is viciously doing everything possible to buck the rider off. The bucks come fast and furious, and sometimes you have no idea where they are even coming from. The audience watches in awe—will s/he get bucked off or not? Like the bull rider, the change agent will experience countless "bucks" and needs to learn to ride it out.

As you embark on your leadership journey as director, superintendent, or head of school, it is highly likely that at some point in your career you will be hired by a school board to initiate significant change. This board is not looking for tweaking or keeping the status quo. They are looking for a significant overhaul to how the school operates. They yearn for the school to be on a new trajectory. The board may not have a clear idea of what that looks like yet (that is your job to help them develop this), but they know they have hired you to be an agent of change - *the change agent!* You are specifically hired to make a profound and impactful difference.

I remember the first time I was offered the change agent role. The excitement and pure joy was overwhelming. I thought, *Finally, I am now empowered to create the optimal school according to my own beliefs and philosophy.* (OK, I was very naïve at the time.) But, after a short period of time relishing in this euphoric state, I was immediately consumed with panic - wait, what is the optimal school? Do I know what the optimal school even looks like? How will we get there? Will I let people down? Or worse, I will get found out that I do not know everything in education! I suddenly began gasping for air.

Fortunately, I have been in this state of exhilaration and then self-doubt and panic before:

- selected to captain numerous rugby teams
- appointed head coach of the Dominican Republic national rugby team
- hired as elementary principal for the first time
- designated to lead a team of educational leaders for school accreditation visits
- chosen to present at conferences
- asked to write a chapter in this book

For me, these types of moments have always brought initial excitement and contentment and then are immediately followed by self-doubt. The responsibility of leadership has always been daunting, and I have never taken it for granted; rather, it inspires me to be the best I can. Why is being a change agent not a smooth experience?

1. While the board might have purposely hired you to be the change agent, this mandate may not have been clearly communicated nor agreed upon by all stakeholders. In this situation you will be immediately confronted with: "Why are we even making changes? We have always done it this way and it works just fine." I am always

dumbfounded by this statement: "We have always done it this way and it works just fine." Yes, having students write lines for inappropriate behavior is a form of punishment that was "done," but I would argue it might not be the best way to effectively address inappropriate behavior.

2. Some school boards do not fully appreciate that change inevitably brings stress and potential conflicts along the way. You need to prepare them for this.

3. Some teachers/administrators are aware you are coming in to make change and are keen on the idea of change. However, they often do not realize that this will affect them and may pull them out of their comfort zone. A couple of examples:
    - Teacher: "Yeah, we need change to be a great school. What do you mean I need to document curriculum? I have it all up here!" (points to head)
    - Curriculum leader: "Yes, we need to document our curriculum. Wait, you mean I must review all the documentation and follow up with teachers to provide professional guidance about their progress on a consistent basis?"

4. Some adamantly refuse change. They like the comfort of status quo, mediocrity, and low expectations. I remember one teacher stating in a meeting, "Why do you have such lofty goals for our school? We are never going to be an 'Ideal' School."

5. In the beginning, no one knows who you truly are, what you believe in, and if what you are saying is just "talking the talk." Trust takes time - remember this!

Okay, at this point, hopefully you understand that being the change agent is empowering and exciting, but it comes with challenges ("bucks"). So, how do you ride the bull?

There are many aspects which contribute to being a successful change agent:

a. A clear and strategic vision
b. Establishing structures to ensure genuine stakeholder voice
c. Identifying faculty leaders and empowering them; encouraging all to lead
d. Authentic relationship building
e. Building a team atmosphere
f. High expectations and accountability
g. An infectiously positive attitude and celebrating successes

However, I believe the underpinning to all of these is leading with integrity. To be a successful change agent, it is imperative you lead with integrity.

Lead with Integrity

An accomplished change agent exudes integrity. So, this may seem like a no-brainer, and you have probably read about leading with integrity in every piece of writing referring to best practice in leadership: "be honest," "follow through," and "do the right thing." It is true, all leaders should aspire to lead with integrity, and most will proclaim they do. Think about it: How many times have you heard a leader share, "I am a strategic thinker, very knowledgeable and experienced in education and best practice, but I struggle at times to lead with integrity." Never, right? However, I would argue that statement exemplifies the concept of integrity. Why? I am going to let you in on a best-kept secret and something most educational leadership articles and books fail to tell you: Leading with integrity is a consistent struggle to do so with fidelity. Now, before you write me off as an unscrupulous and dishonest person, let me explain. In theory, this seems straightforward - be honest, follow through, and do the right thing, but doing so can be challenging.

Let's start with the complexities of being *honest*. The school was moving forward with a new educational initiative and a person from the leadership team, who I was just becoming acquainted with and trying to build a relationship with (I was the newbie), asked if they could lead it. "Absolutely," I replied. *Note to self: Always preview new school initiative presentations if you do not know the person well.* Unfortunately, the presentation was poorly organized and executed. Following up after the presentation, the person came into my office beaming with pride, confidently sharing how well it went and thanking me for the opportunity. They then asked me for feedback. Remember, this is a new colleague who I was trying to build a positive relationship with, and they seem so pleased with their "accomplishment." It would have been much easier to agree with them, say nothing, and strengthen our relationship (in the short term). Or I could be honest with them. What would you do in that moment?

What about being honest with your board chair? While it seems to be obvious that the head and board chair need to have a close relationship, I am surprised by the number of heads of school who do not place a greater emphasis on it or ignore it altogether. Being honest with your board chair also means you need to highlight that you are fallible and vulnerable at times too. This can be challenging to share with a board chair because we, heads, become indoctrinated into believing we must always exude invincibility and guru-like wisdom to garner the board chair's confidence. Openly sharing your mistakes, challenges, or need of support (at times) with your boss seems counterproductive to ensuring longevity in your position. However, by doing so, you build trust and demonstrate integrity. If the board chair knows they can count on you to be forthright, regardless of the scenario, they will trust in you. Regardless of my initial apprehensions to share mistakes or challenges I was grappling with; I have never regretted communicating these with the board chair. Why? Sharing mistakes or where I have failed lets the board chair know I recognize my errors and know that I am human (albeit somewhat of a bull rider). It also exudes humility, which should be a mandatory characteristic for any head. When I disclose what challenges I am facing, it gives the board chair better insight into my work, provides them an opportunity to share solutions, or at the very least, enables them to better understand how or why certain decisions were made. Additionally, and selfishly, sharing my struggles with someone else can be cathartic. Remember, it can get lonely at the top. My experience has proven, time and time again, that healthy and trusting board chair and head relationships rely heavily upon honest communication. Share the good, bad, and ugly so they are never caught off guard and never have a reason to not trust in you. This trust will, in turn, empower you to make the change needed.

Next, a change agent will certainly face situations where expectations are set but not met. A leader of integrity will *follow through* when expectations are not met. Unless you have a twisted desire to reprimand others (if you do, please get out of the profession now!), following through; having a difficult conversation with someone regarding not meeting expectations is never easy. As you likely know, in the international setting, it is quite common for administrators and teachers to also have personal relationships. Imagine having a great social evening with your friend, who is also a teacher at your school, on Friday, and then having to sit him down on Tuesday morning for a serious meeting regarding not meeting his professional expectations. Sure, it would have been much easier to let it slide and not follow through, but that would not be acting with integrity. *Side note: If it is a true friend, they will appreciate your courage to have the difficult conversation.*

Now, if you *do the right thing*, how can that be difficult? I was once at a school where we had a teacher who was an absolute gem of a human being, with an incredibly kind soul. She was sweet, well-known, and revered by many in the community - truly, she had saint - like status. The problem was she was hired over twenty years prior yet was not actually a qualified teacher, her decision-making skills had diminished greatly over the years, and ultimately, the learning environment for students was far from optimal. After much time, action plans, and support from many people, the grim reality set in. I had to let Santa Claus know this would be her final year. I felt sick about it, but it was *the right thing to do* for our students. Fortunately, she took the news like a champion, and after the shock wore off, the community was comfortable with the decision because I had earned their trust over time, and they were confident in my integrity. Still, *doing the right thing* was not straightforward, nor easy.

Leading with integrity (not just talking about it), especially in the first year of being a change agent, will bring you a tremendous amount of stress in the short term. Why? Earned belief in your integrity is not a luxury afforded the brand-new change agent.

As a new head (and change agent), I was once faced with letting a teacher go mid-year. This decision was very straightforward based on the circumstances and evidence presented. Anyone who knew the truth would have acted in the same manner. The challenge: It was early in my tenure at the school (people were still analyzing and evaluating my integrity) and the "nice" teacher was publicly disparaging me and began communicating false narratives about me, my leadership, and why she was let go. My character and fundamental values were questioned/attacked, but I stayed true to my integrity and refused to divulge the highly confidential situation for the sake of students, the teacher herself, and the stability of the school. Did some of the disparaging comments hurled at me hurt? Sure. Was my developing reputation inaccurately judged at the time because, unbeknownst to them, I exuded integrity? Certainly. Would sharing the actual reason the person was abruptly let go have made my life easier in the short term? Absolutely. However, I would have compromised my integrity and others would have been negatively affected. Leading with genuine integrity goes unnoticed at times and some will never know when you have been an exemplar of integrity. This can be incredibly challenging and, frankly, lonely, but you are charged with upholding what is best for your students and community, not your feelings.

As a change agent, you may be faced with the decision of whether to compromise your integrity for a short-term "win." With all my leadership teams, I have stressed the importance of having rigorous discourse in our meetings but, once an agreement has been made, the team must publicly support the decision (unless there are safety or ethical concerns, of course!). *Side note: The only exception to this is if I have had to make an unpopular decision to "do the right thing." In this situation, I will take full responsibility for the decision.* So, a decision about an initiative was made by the leadership team. I, personally, was not in favor of the policy and conveyed my opposition during our discussions; however, there were no safety nor ethical concerns and it did not compromise my fundamental beliefs, so I acquiesced. Once shared with the faculty, a teacher became extremely upset about the policy and confronted an administrative leader about the decision. Ironically, it was the same administrative leader who strongly supported and promoted adoption of the policy. Shockingly, the administrative leader not only discarded publicly supporting the "team" decision but also shared they, too, did not personally believe in the policy. Rather, they inaccurately divulged it was the head's (my) decision. The teacher then confronted me about the policy, and specifically questioned if I had single-handedly mandated the decision as she was told. So, a supposedly trusted administrative partner has just thrown you under the bus regarding the policy that they created (something you did not support in the first place) to be liked. How would you manage this? It would have been much easier to act without integrity and even somewhat "just" to highlight the administrator's dishonesty;

however, leading with integrity and following through with publicly supporting leadership team decisions, I protected the administrator and honestly shared with the teacher that we make decisions as a leadership team. Did the teacher leave feeling disgruntled and that it was solely my mandated decision? Most likely. Did I maintain my integrity? Absolutely.

As a head of school, your integrity is always questioned. This is why leading with integrity, especially as a newly minted change agent, takes courage and strength. The bull rider needs to absorb violent and painful bucks yet not back down, panic or lose composure, and stick to the goal of riding the bull. People watching will never fully appreciate the excruciating pain the bull rider experiences during certain bucks; rather, they are just watching to see if the bull rider can manage the bucks (even ones the spectators do not see) and stay on the bull. All school stakeholders are watching the change agent from a distance and can never be fully privy to all the "bucks" occurring, nor how s/he is managing those "bucks." Trust me, as a change agent, it is much easier to initially lead *without* integrity and to just try to please everyone and steer clear of conflict so people like you. Problem is, this is short lived and, if you were making decisions to be a pleaser instead of doing what is right, you will eventually get found out and be "bucked off." Leading with integrity is the ideal, and people will be scrutinizing and evaluating your actions to see if you do; but ironically, many will never see when you do lead in this manner. It is the cruel reality, with rewards that only you get to savor.

I assure you that leading with integrity will ultimately bring you self-assurance and a sense of peace. For the bull rider, it is like gripping and tightly clinging to the flat braided rope while riding the bull. That grip must be secure, and, if it is, the bull rider actually becomes emboldened by it and there is a greater chance s/he will have a successful ride. Picture for a moment the bull rider without the grip - arms and body flailing everywhere before being unceremoniously bucked off. Similarly, the change agent who compromises their integrity will find themselves floundering and, inevitably, unsuccessful.

Before I come off as too pompous and/or self-righteous, I want to be clear that I have certainly slipped at times. For example, there have been a few difficult conversations I did not have with people with the hope things would just get better. You know what? It never did get better, and, many times, the issue only worsened. I have never regretted staying true to my integrity and having a difficult conversation, but on numerous occasions I have regretted when I shied away from having the necessary difficult conversation.

Hopefully, by now you realize leading with integrity is the ideal, but, especially as a change agent, it is a constant struggle to do so with fidelity. Being new, your trust equity with all stakeholders is initially minimal, and it will take time for them to realize you lead with integrity - remember this! The key is you stay the course and not compromise your integrity because of a seductive, short-term win. Again, many times actions you take that exude integrity may never be recognized nor made known; however, these actions will help you sleep better at night.

The good news is, when people do realize you lead with integrity, they become ardent supporters/colleagues/teammates and real change can occur. Let's go back to the bull rider analogy. The ride becomes even more impressive later when it is revealed that the bull rider cracked their ribs on the first buck, yet never swayed from the goal - it is inspiring. Similarly, when people realize, over time, that you were unjustly disparaged or accused yet always maintained your integrity throughout, only then is when your integrity is truly appreciated/admired. Simultaneously, you earn the trust equity that empowers significant change to happen.

When people fully believe in your integrity, a mind shift occurs.

There is a comforting and enveloping sense of relief, stability, and calmness when they recognize you lead with integrity. They know you are earnest with your vision and follow through. From my experience, this inspires people and, in turn, enables a greater sense of commitment from everyone. A common theme I have heard from teachers: I questioned your motives initially and I was not necessarily a fan of yours, but it became very evident your integrity never wavered, and I began to trust in you and our direction. Your conviction helped me be a better professional and collaborator and motivated me to commit to the vision.

When people see you "walk the walk," they become excited and inspired to contribute to an authentic and impactful journey. Now, they are ready to join the change agent in significant school improvement.

Being a change agent is exciting and has been one of my greatest professional accomplishments. It has also been one of the greatest professional challenges I have ever faced. It is imperative you lead with integrity to be successful; however, it is a constant struggle to do so with fidelity.

So, clutch the flat braided rope, be mindful of the bucks, and enjoy the ride!

About Dr. Colin Brown

Dr. Brown is the Head of School at the American School in Taichung, Taiwan and currently the Board President of the Council of Administrators of Taiwan Expatriate Schools (CATES). He has over 25 years in the education field and has held administrative positions or taught in Canada, China, Guatemala, Hungary, Vietnam, and the Dominican Republic. Dr. Brown has presented at leadership conferences in Kentucky, Atlanta, Medellin, Abu Dhabi and Cairo on innovations in curriculum development, standards-based grading and reporting and a unique teacher professional growth program. He has had numerous educational articles published and has led many workshops for teachers and administrators on new initiatives in education. Dr. Brown has frequently led or served on Cognia/AdvancED accreditation visits around the world (since 2011), and he has also served on or led accreditation visits for CIS/WASC/NEASC. Dr. Brown's family is truly international as he is Canadian, his wife Laura (also an educator) is Australian, his eldest daughter Keira was born in China and his youngest daughter Maya was born in Guatemala.

12

Authentic Learning through Tackling Complexity Systemically: Deeper Learning, Better World

Community of Care and Support for Students

Dr. Michael Johnston

It's a familiar sight at many of the international schools I've worked at: students and teachers become passionate about an issue, implement a well-intentioned but less than systemic plan, and ultimately the initiative loses steam or does not produce the desired results. They are not high-stakes projects, but shouldn't school be the place students learn how to go from caring about creating change to being able to do so in impactful ways? Students learn about these critical issues throughout the school day but often are not allocated the time, tools, and support needed to tackle them in meaningful ways. Whether it is a club, a class, or a personal passion project, students have the capacity and desire to create a better future; all we need to do in schools is create the time, teach the tools, mentor, and step out of the way.

A student council was taking on the issue of trash being left in the cafeteria by students. It is a very typical scenario in K–12 private international schools, in my experience. They were doomed to repeat the pitfalls of many other student groups by providing solutions riddled with unintended consequences. They immediately wanted to act by making posters, creating a video, placing more teachers on duty, and buying more garbage cans for the cafeteria. All of these "solutions" have unintended consequences that cost money, divert time from higher leverage things, and do not really make a long-term sustainable change. Once they used a more systemic approach to expose mental models and systems connections, they had a much more robust plan to tackle this reoccurring issue. Their first ideas would create more trash, waste people's time, and take away precious minutes that teachers should be spending doing something else of higher leverage than being a trash guard - all unintended consequences of good intentions. When they worked through the process using visual mapping, the systems iceberg, and a cyclical process, they came up with a plan to work on the mental models of the parents.

Effective change agents need to conceptually understand change and build a robust toolbox filled with systemic and complexity tools for change. By going through a more robust process, the council realized that these students do not clean up after themselves anywhere else in their lives, so why would they at school? It really wasn't about the system of garbage and waste; it was about people's mental models. Their campaign, nicknamed in private "you're raising a slob," turned into a robust life skills program launched at parent coffee mornings as they helped parents realize that their own children did not have the life skills to go off to university on their own and they were enabling this behavior. Students, teachers, leaders, parents, and all stakeholders within an international school community can understand systems, reveal mental models, and ultimately create long-lasting and meaningful change. Whether it's a change effort by a director on a macro scale, or a micro project to reduce waste in school, the concepts, skills, character traits, and tools are the same. The best part of all is that in the process of doing so, the learning is rich, personalized, and character building beyond anything we could expect in a traditional school setting. Deeper learning and a better future—I cannot think of two stronger reasons for schools to exist.

Educating toward a more positive future means facilitating learning that is connected to our global reality in a way that is engaging, thought provoking, character developing, and skill building. Ultimately, schools around the world would be fostering global citizens who not only embrace the complexities but also have the will and skills to create something better. Instead of fearing complexity and checking out, we want generations of young people to be excited by complexity and dig into the mess. Systemic approaches are the key to both deeper learning and embracing complexity for better solutions to today's most difficult issues. A systemic, connected approach will help prepare students for a future that is unknown and ever changing. The traditional factory model of kindergarten to grade 12 (K–12) education is not serving the learning needs of a new generation of complexity thinkers and practitioners. There are many factors that hold schools back from progressing and ultimately embracing the complexity of the world. The systems and structures that surround education have been embedded for generations and this makes it very challenging to shift. Antiquated grading and reporting practices, knowledge driven assessments and a focus on ranking rather than personal growth are just a few that keep the learning in silos. It is systemic thinking and practices that will not only transform learning experiences for students but also lead to identifying leverage points of change from within and around the K–12 education system itself.

As a school leader, I have experienced the transformation these approaches can have on all stakeholders. Senior leaders can impact the outcomes systemically for student learning, school operations, teacher development, parent engagement, local connections, and global impact. School leaders can foster the same skills and approaches in teachers and students to tackle local and global issues. It is a daunting but exciting charge we have as leaders, but the outcomes are worth the time invested for learning and for our planet. School leaders need to be chameleons as you adapt to your surroundings to create opportunities that make sense in your context.

At Frankfurt International School, we started a student leadership program with fourth- to 11th grade students by partnering with The Jump Foundation and Inspire Citizens. The term *student leadership* resonated with our community and got it off the ground; the students have now named it the FIS Changemakers, as they feel this is really what they are trying to do, create change locally and globally. The students are leading by experiencing, and then facilitating workshops for community members on systems, change, and mental models. They have learned about economies of the future with Doughnut Economics, Circular economic models, how to use systems mapping, root cause trees, the sustainability compass, a systems iceberg model, and many new ways of thinking. These skills, tools, concepts, and character traits that the students are honing are the same that it takes to transform schools on a systemic level. As the students work on a longer-term project to foster the creation of change agents year after year at FIS, they also apply these new skills and tools to their own passion projects in service learning in the upper school or as an action step from an inquiry unit in elementary school.

A group of Grade 4 and 5 students have used the changemaking skills and tools to create a kindness group to foster well-being in the upper elementary school. Middle and high school students apply the learning in their service learning projects, such as Amnesty International and the Clean Water Initiative. Beyond their own projects, the students have decided to host a global conference and have plans for a long-term program of upskilling and support to impact FIS and change the world. They see the conference as a catalyst within the FIS community and want to foster regional collaboration for tackling our most pressing issues. From their impactful work, many opportunities have arisen that were unexpected, which is often the case when we allow students to take the lead. Our Changemakers have been invited to run workshops for teachers in the region and beyond, been interviewed on podcasts (share.transistor.fm/s/1731ce8a) and been asked to present at a regional board meeting for where they see the best leverage to help schools take authentic action; and they are doing this on their own time—no grades, no credit, they are just motivated for good. My next step as a leader in the school is to embed these kinds of opportunities throughout the school day to ensure all ages and all students have access to such amazing opportunities to follow their passions and learn how to create impact. It's an example of dynamic change plans embedded in dynamic change plans.

In the last three international schools that I have been fortunate enough to be a part of, we all worked together to understand the systems that surrounded us. I recall an amazing moment of clarity when a teacher came to see me after we had played the systems triangles game as a staff to understand causal connections and change. This systemic simulation has participants standing in a circle and then choosing two others in the circle that they will stay in a triangle with once the facilitator says "go." What initially participants think will be chaos transforms into a flowing dance of parts and connections. To live the experience of a system with one simple rule and many parts helps people understand what happens when you change the rules or manipulate a part of the system to create a desired change. *We* played the game as we were undergoing some key changes for assessment, but this teacher saw the bigger picture quickly. He came to me and apologized for complaining about the teaching schedule he had been assigned at the beginning of the year. He stated that he wished he had taken me up on the offer to be involved last June as the whole community was invited to see the large puzzle that is classrooms, courses, students, time blocks, teachers, and so on. He realized what the balcony view looked like and that his piece was just one of many pulling on each other. He stated, "understanding systems will relieve some stress for me." We have an amazing opportunity to bring renewed meaning to schools, drive learning deeper through a systemic approach, and ultimately cocreate the world we wish to have moving toward the future.

An elementary teaching team in an international school was working on creating deep inquiry units from what previously were very linear approaches to disciplines. The toughest change was what to give up, making space to have students truly inquire and take meaningful action because it takes time to do so. Board members would ask questions like, "How can we be doing more of this inquiry thing when my child doesn't even know Christopher Columbus and the dates of exploration?" The grade-level team had done a Greek play for years - great costumes and parents attended, but it took a tremendous amount of time to prepare. When asked about what the students were learning conceptually, what competencies were built, and what character had been fostered, the teachers had trouble articulating specifics. It's not that the play was a bad thing; it just was not the highest leverage thing that could be done with their time. There was unrest when the play did not happen, but when the students instead hosted a learning share with the community on the concept of democracy and created a student–peer mediation group because of what they learned, the impact was clear. The parents saw first-hand the impact this deeper learning had on their kids, the teachers were able to really allow students to take the lead on their learning, and the students themselves were able to articulate clearly what they had learned and how they had grown, not to mention the impact they were having on their community. Sometimes we need to ride the rough waves to get to the calm waters. It is often difficult for some to see in the planning stages or during change and it is not until the lived experience when the penny drops for understanding. For teachers and other adults, the concepts of systems, change, and mental models are the same as what we should be doing with students for authentic action.

Students were very clear in their feedback to me as I worked with an independent school to help them implement more authentic learning and for the students to grow in intrinsic motivation. They had state testing to adhere to, a course grade, and independent time for inquiry and exploration. Unfortunately, this places the students under tremendous strain as they stated a lack of motivation for the inquiry time because they had grades and testing to do well on. The school was attempting to do both but living a frenzied existence of extrinsic and intrinsic motivation. The emphasis was clearly placed on the testing and grades and until the purpose was made clear the intentions of the exploration time would struggle. Leaders need to think, plan, and act systemically to create the authentic learning we wish to see. The students are ready to tackle complexity and take meaningful action, but leaders need to create scenarios where there is time for both satisfying the system for next steps in schools and authentic learning.

What Could Learning Look Like if It Were Systemic?

K–12 schools, engaged in their local and global communities, provide connection, motivation, and fulfillment for all stakeholders. Systemic and authentic approaches are not new to the world of education, and the research exists to show the impact on learning. Place-based education as shared by Williams (2003) is "where the community provides a context for learning, student work focuses on community needs and interests, and community members serve as resources and partners in every aspect of teaching and learning" (p. i). The trash in the cafeteria is an example of using an authentic situation for deep learning and application. These opportunities are all around us; they simply need to be incorporated into the learning flow. The school facility itself offers thousands of learning opportunities, whether it be a waste project, carbon exploration, or energy audit. The fourth- and fifth-grade kindness group is applying their learning

131

from an inquiry unit and creating a stronger community.

Associated with place-based education, problem- or project-based learning (PBL) is when the student's learning process is facilitated by the identification of a specific problem to work on (Barell, 2007). "The students' tasks are to identify the current state of their knowledge, identify what further information is needed, seek out that information, analyze and evaluate the information, and make plans for action vis-a-vis the case study" (Askell-Williams, H., et al, 2007, p. 240). Thomas (2000) did a comprehensive review of the research on PBL over 20 years ago and found learning improved when using a PBL approach compared to other instructional methods. Holm (2011) reviewed the effectiveness of PBL in K–12 learning and found similar results over ten years after the work of Thomas (2000).

Research clearly indicates that PBL is beneficial, with positive outcomes including increases in levels of student engagement, heightened interest in content, more robust development of problem-solving strategies, and greater depth of learning and transfer of skills to new situations. There is a growing number of schools engaged in the conversation about PBL; to be successful, it is important to ensure the proper conditions with multiple sources and organizations available to aid in this process. The Buck Institute for Education (http://bie.org/) is one of the leaders in providing support, but there are many organizations with all the tools necessary for successful implementation. PBL is one example of how to have students authentically learning, but do not get bogged down by the Edujargon of all the competing initiatives that have the same goals - be the chameleon for your community.

The question most widely asked is about sacrificing academic results by learning in a different way. The Knowledge in Action Efficacy study over two years (Rosefsky, 2021) aimed to find out if using a PBL approach could both give a deeper conceptual understanding and produce good results on external assessments for Advanced Placement. Their findings showed equal and, in most cases, better results on the AP exams for students engaged in this approach. In some cases, students performed significantly better, especially those with more diverse learning needs. At least 80 percent of the students in the study stated the greatest value was the ability to apply what they have learned to their lives outside the classroom. Place-based learning and PBL require a systemic approach to be successful; they are examples of how to implement education for a sustainable future within the current system. Tackling local and global issues requires knowledge about all systems conditions, from economic to natural to social. The strategies, support, and research for learning in a more connected and holistic way exist globally, but what happens next for K–12 schools is the bigger question. Whether a school is calling it PBL, CAS, Service Learning, Passion Projects, Capstone, or the plethora of other terminology for deep learning, the trickiest barrier to implementation is not what to do or how to do it, it's how to make the space. Kevin Bartlett of the Common Ground Collaborative often refers to "the to don't list" and how it's just as important as the to-do list. I have worked with schools that cannot figure what to or how to stop doing things that are not high leverage for learning. Schools can be married to these things that have always just happened for years.

To foster innovation and creativity, a school I worked with moved forward with plans to create an innovation program. What I learned was that the word *innovation* means many things to many people and the idea of student-led versus teacher-led learning was scary to many teachers, students, and parents. Many stakeholders really wanted to know exactly what would be done in this innovation space and what classes will be there. That gave me the understanding that it wasn't about the space; it was about people's mental models toward schooling itself. The big idea was to create a space where students would use digital and product design to create a better world, but the *why* was not clear from the beginning. We created innovation classes as pilots and the students started to thrive through their own cycles of design, failure, retooling, and the link. Questions arose: How will this be assessed? Where is the grade? What will we not do while we are creating and proto-typing what we did before? The challenge was immense, but the intrinsic drive from students to innovate and try to be creative drove the transformation forward. K–12 schools do not need a fancy lab with tools and tech equipment that is still led by the adult in all aspects. The world does not need another pencil holder, never mind 30 of them from students following instructions from a manual and using tools in class. Real-world learning is available always and everywhere; it is a matter of giving students the opportunity to do so and getting things out of their way to allow the learning to be deep, intentional, and meaningful. I use the same tools and concepts to transform school experiences that I teach to students to tackle their own complex issues - they are no different.

A Grade 8 student who had taken on a lead role in student leadership after learning about change, systems, and mental models in Singapore since Grade 6 said to me, "Mr. J., now that I see in systems, I can't unsee systems, they are everywhere." I asked him how he felt about that, and he stated, "It's amazing. I am understanding how the world works much better, but sometimes it can be overwhelming too." As a school leader from within the system and as an external consultant to many schools globally, I have been fortunate to work with dedicated, caring teachers, leaders, board members, students, and parents. The desire to set students up for success in their future, open doors, and give them the skills to follow their passions exists the world over. My work through Compass Education has not only allowed me to consolidate my own learning but to also help thousands of people along the way to tackle complexity themselves. What is now required is support internally and externally to systemically transform antiquated practices and remove the barriers to deep, connected, meaningful learning for all ages. I hold great hope that this is not only possible on a large scale, but it can happen faster than we may believe. I believe this is true because of the countless examples I have witnessed of educators finding leverage in their day-to-day practice and the growing number of new school models and approaches being created and implemented around the world.

There appears to be a will on the part of many K–12 educators to facilitate the kind of learning that gives greater purpose and growth of skills and character, what is required is to find the way. Traditional content-driven curriculum and assessing students on memory recall in standardized ways is not what today's learner needs. A more connected, student-driven, and emergent curriculum will create generations of deep thinkers and systemic practitioners with strong values and character. Not only do the learning progressions for students need to be more systemic rather than linear, integrated, and connected across disciplines, but the education system itself needs to be challenged to do so. Educators around the world are seeking to open a future of possibilities for their students and provide them with the necessary knowledge and understanding, skills, and character development that will lead to future success. The long-standing linear constructs in K–12 schools are being challenged in many ways from both internal and external pressure. It is seeking a move toward more systemic models in schools for both improved student learning and improved planetary balance for the natural and human systems. Striving toward deeper understanding and action toward a better future in K–12 schools, being systems literate to tackle complex issues, and having tools to move forward on these complex interrelated issues will help K–12 education contribute profoundly toward creating a flourishing future for all. Our children need it, they deserve it, and our future depends upon it.

Askell-Williams, H., et al (2007). Teacher education students reflections on how problem-based learning has changed their mental models about teaching and learning. *The Teacher Educator*, 42(4), 237–263.

Barell, J. (2007). *Problem-based learning: An inquiry approach*. Thousand Oaks, CA: Corwin Press.

Buck Institute for Education. (2021). *Project Based Learning*. https://www.pblworks.org

Holm, M. (2011). Project-based instruction: A review of the literature on effectiveness in prekindergarten through 12th grade classrooms. *River Academic Journal*, 7(2). Retrieved from http://bie.org/object/document/project_based_learning_a_review_of_the_literature_on_effectiveness

Rosefsky Saavedra, A. et al. (2021). Knowledge in action efficacy study over two years. Los Angeles, CA: USCDornsife Center for economic and social research.

Thomas, J. W. (2000). *A review of research on project-based learning*. San Rafael, CA: Autodesk Foundation.

Williams, D. T. (2003). *The place-based learning portfolio*. Washington, DC: The Rural School and Community Trust.

About Dr. Michael Johnston

Mike Johnston is the Assistant Head at Frankfurt International School. He has lead workshops and keynoted for teachers and administrators around the world on learning innovation, sustainability, building global competence, deep personalized curriculum K-12 and how service learning should not just be what you do, but who you are as a school. Mike is a proud member of the Common Ground Collaborative advisory council seeking to transform learning in schools globally. He is also a member of the Compass Education team which is a growing community of passionate educators aiming to equip schools as learning communities to educate and act for a sustainable future through systems thinking and practice. He has dedicated much of his time to not only ensuring students are properly prepared for the world's most pressing issues but that they have the skills and desire to take action. With his Doctorate in Organizational Systems Mike helps to inspire and lead schools through times of change and educational transformation. Please visit https://www.johnstonmike.com/ for more information.

13

Lessons from Women Leaders: Creating Schools Where Females - and the Schools They Lead - Can Thrive

Equity and Cultural Responsiveness

Bridget McNamer

I formally launched *Sidecar Counsel* in the spring of 2020, blissfully unaware that COVID-19 was about to upend the personal and professional realities of my target clientele: women leaders in international schools. At the time, my growing coaching practice - a side hustle up to that point - centered on helping women leaders navigate a leadership search process that was designed by and for men. As a leadership search consultant with Search Associates for seven years and having played a role in fifty-plus leadership searches for schools all over the world, I had seen the process up close. From sourcing to on-boarding, it was stacked against women. No wonder so few made it to senior leadership roles, particularly beyond the primary school stage. Recent statistics from the Council on International Schools, pulled from a survey of 175 international schools, found that 25 percent of these schools are headed by women and 75 percent by men - and this despite 69 percent of teachers in these schools being female.

As these statistics reveal, and as my *Sidecar* metaphor suggests, being a woman seeking leadership opportunities in international schools (and serving in those roles) is like riding a motorcycle on a mountain road: exhilarating and adventurous… and lonely and at times bewildering and unnerving. And, like the image of an international school leader, too many people think of mountain-bound motorcyclists as male. My initial approach with women leaders was to help them navigate their motorcycles through this male-designed landscape, to be able to compete and perform on those male-centered terms.

Now, a full eighteen months into my *Sidecar* coaching adventure, I find myself immersed in, and fascinated by, a different perspective on women and leadership, drawn mainly from my coaching conversations with women leaders in international schools though also from a range of resources: studies, webinars, news stories, random reading, nature. COVID has, of course, been the game changer. It has revealed both how valuable female leadership attributes are, particularly in times of both acute and prolonged crisis, but also how vulnerable the international school community is to losing its female leaders if they are not appropriately supported. And it is giving me insights into ways international schools can adapt (and in some cases, wholesale change) to better support female leaders and, indeed, allow them to thrive. It will take bold and daring leadership—from boards/ownership bodies, leadership teams, parents, and the entire support infrastructure for international schools—to shift the leadership landscape so that female leadership attributes can be brought to the fore. The survival of our schools depends on this.

Why female leadership attributes? At the risk of oversimplifying and stereotyping (many men embody these attributes; not all females do), some traits associated as female that have emerged as noteworthy—media reports and my own observations are my main sources here—during the COVID crisis include the following:

- **Risk-consciousness**. Decisions that prioritize people's health and well-being over economic factors.
- **Clear and decisive communication**. Even when the news is grim or the answers elusive, people appreciate real information and clarity behind decision-making.
- **Connection rooted in empathy**. Leaders who demonstrate care and concern for community members during times of crisis tend to have stronger loyalty as a result.
- **Collaborative mindset**. Reliance on teams, tendency toward inclusion, and curiosity about dissenting viewpoints leads to more robust responses to crises.
- **Humility**. Leaders who show vulnerability while making courageous decisions generally gain the confidence of their constituents - yes, even during times of crisis and when the outcome is uncertain.

Along with these positive traits come other, less healthy attributes: a propensity to try to please everyone, to extend oneself beyond what is humanly possible, to sacrifice one's personal health and well-being in order to support that of others, to try to achieve perfection in an imperfect world, to avoid conflict, to suppress personal aspirations. These attributes, if gone unchecked, can lead straight to burnout.

How can you as a school leader and we as an international school community recognize and elevate the positive attributes of female leadership while also building the supportive infrastructure to keep these less healthy propensities at bay? I will call on my direct coaching and consulting experiences as well as the rich trove of information that has come about women leaders and COVID to illustrate the four fundamental leadership lessons I believe are elemental to support women leaders more effectively in international schools—and thereby ensure greater, more sustainable success for schools. Even as we move past the initial, acute stages of the COVID era, leading in international schools will continue to involve navigating crises of one form or another as well as tricky, uncertain passages that are the nature of the future we are inheriting. This future can look a lot brighter for everyone if we can make space for women's voices, perspectives, and attributes, and if we can make schools spaces where females can thrive.

Lesson 1: Ensure females in your school community feel safe from physical, sexual, and psychological harm

Our international school community came together quickly and decisively to address child protection concerns in response to prominent pedophilia scandals that came to light in 2015. At this point, any school that does not have a child protection policy and attendant protocols is ineligible for accreditation and should be avoided at all costs by anyone concerned about the welfare of children (i.e., anyone involved in any way with education). Women are also a highly vulnerable group when it comes to physical, sexual, and psychological safety. Too often I've been on the other end of a call with a female educator or leader who has been solicited, groped, or physically assaulted (by someone either in the school community or outside of it), and who either doesn't know her school's protocol to address this, doesn't trust it will serve her needs, or has received inadequate response to her complaint. The burden of proof generally rests with the female victim in these instances. This is a tough battle to fight, especially without policies and protocols in place. What will it take to bring this issue the attention it deserves?

Then there are the daily "microaggressions" that women face, whether it is interruptions, patronizing or sexualizing comments, or other cuts to her worth or individuality. Many women are confident enough to let these slights roll off their backs (insert hard eye roll here), though this is at the cost of respect for the perpetrator. When this type of behavior is tolerated by leadership, it sends a clear message about school culture and values. That's not a recipe for an environment where women (or really anyone) will thrive.

> **Suggested Actions**: Develop policies and protocols around harassment. Include women and vulnerable groups in their development. Communicate about them early and often. Abide by them. Check in with females regularly to see if they are feeling safe. Listen to them.

Lesson 2: Support women's health, well-being, and family responsibilities

Women tend to neglect their own health to focus on that of others - their family members (those living with them and those far away), their students/staff/school community members, and their friends. When I ask my coaching clients what they are doing to support their own health, too often the question is deflected, or I simply get a blank stare. The "always on" culture of many schools means that women leaders feel they simply don't have time to address personal health issues or to fit in regular exercise to their schedules.

Here's the reality: if women don't move their own health and well-being (physical and psychological/emotional) up the chain of their priorities, they will soon be drawing on an empty well and entering a burnout stage.

Then there's the fact that premenopausal women (including most of the female students in our schools) have monthly periods, which are manageable for many and three-plus days per month of heavy bleeding and excruciating cramps for some. As a baseline, can schools please make feminine hygiene products easily available for the female members of the school community? A step further: educate all members of the school community about this aspect of being female. It's something to celebrate and honor. It keeps our species going! It is also something that can be very difficult for females. It is certainly not something about which they should ever feel ashamed.

Then there's menopause. Most of us can be forgiven for not understanding what this really implies because there seems to be a global code of silence around the topic. News flash: menopause affects *all women* at some point in their lives if they live to be at least 60. Women at the height of their leadership careers fall squarely in the range of the menopause years. As with menstruation, menopause symptoms can range from mild to agonizing. Imagine juggling the multiple responsibilities of school leadership while experiencing sudden and intense hot spells, inexplicable mood swings, deep fatigue, foggy memory, and the accompanying feelings of shame and embarrassment that comes from not knowing or not admitting this could be the unspeakable menopause?

In this general category, leaders (of any gender) with children or wishing to bear or adopt children, and those with care responsibilities for distant family members, face a whole other set of issues related to well-being. Note the "always on" culture comment above, add to that the empathetic tendencies of many female leaders, mix that with the actual duties involved in caring for dependents and loved ones along with the attendant emotional labor that comes as part of the package, and you get a rich stress cocktail.

Schools that recognize these issues and provide appropriate support for their female leaders (and entire school communities) in addressing them are likely to be rewarded with greater energy and greater loyalty from these leaders.

Suggested Actions: Develop and instill a culture of well-rounded well-being for *all* members of your school community. Encourage leaving work at work and preserving home life for personal priorities and pursuits (including regular exercise). As above, have feminine hygiene products freely available at school. Have resources about menstruation and menopause available. Ensure that family and personal leave policies reflect best practice.

Lesson 3: Hire, develop, promote, and pay women leaders equitably with men

It continues to amaze (and depress) me that we *still* need to make the case for gender equity in leadership in the international school community. Is there something inherent to men that make them better suited to leading in an international school than women? If so, I've never heard a convincing explanation for that. (Some of my coaching clients say they've been told that women are "too emotional" to lead schools, or that they lack the capacity to be decisive. To which I say: "Really? Hmm. Let's discuss that further.") Why is it that a profession (education) that has traditionally drawn more females than males is so overwhelmingly predominated by male leaders? And why does that remain so stubbornly the case even in the year 2022?

Resources making the case for equity in school leadership (gender and other identifiers) are in ample supply and easily available for school leadership teams, boards, ownership bodies, and recruiting firms. Accreditation agencies are taking this issue on board. Consultants are ready to help schools figure this out. What this will take is commitment by schools (and the supporting ecosystem around them) to take this issue seriously, to commit to it with real goals and timelines (like next recruiting cycle). There is simply no excuse not to do so.

Achieving equity in leadership roles will be a game-changer, though it isn't the end game. Female leaders (and aspiring leaders) also need equal access to, and active encouragement to pursue, professional development opportunities and internal promotions. Lining up mentors, sponsors, allies, and other champions to support these women's aspirations will also send a signal that your school is eager to invest in its leadership talent.

Then there is the issue of pay equity. Even after seven years of consulting on leadership searches for international schools, I have found myself flabbergasted by the sometimes-yawning gaps between what male and female leaders earn for the same position. One of my coaching clients who recently took a new head of school position found out that her replacement at her former school - a male - was earning *twice* what she'd earned, and this even though she has a doctoral degree (he does not) and six years more head of school experience than he does. What?! Most recent data from the Council of International Schools (CIS) (year?)shows a $8,500 pay gap between male and female heads of school among their membership.

Paying women equitably with men signals that your school values their professional experience and attributes - not as *female professionals*, as *professionals*. When a woman performs the same job as a man, or a different job of equal or comparable value, she should be paid what a man would be paid.

Importantly, CIS has also raised the issue about overall compensation, which includes benefits. Clearly, these also need to be taken into account to give a more complete picture of equity, or lack thereof, between males and females. Anecdotally, I can say with confidence that women receive less than their male counterparts because they tend to avoid negotiating their contracts. Even seasoned female heads of school haven't done it - ever. For many it just hasn't occurred to them that contracts are negotiable (why did men get that memo and women didn't?). For

145

others, they are culturally conditioned to accept what's been offered to them, to be grateful for it, and to not ask questions or—ask for *more* (cue the porridge scene from the musical *Oliver*).

I've been coaching women leaders on the importance of negotiating contracts, not just from the perspective of pay equity, but to (1) demonstrate that they know their worth (including to themselves), (2) identify and ask for benefits that will allow them to be more successful on the job (which serves the school well), and (3) prove that they have negotiation skills, which are hugely important for any leader. Hiring committees can set the stage for this by indicating they are expecting negotiation; that their initial offer is the first step and is a basis for ongoing discussion, with the goal of a mutually agreeable set of terms and conditions that will serve all parties well.

A well-negotiated contract can make the difference between short-term failure and longer-term success on the job. This is where it's important to make the distinction between equity and equality. Men and women may have equitable compensation packages that look different in composition. Indeed, compensation packages can and should be personalized to the individual leader - whether male or female - and reflect what will most support that person's success on the job. This can reflect factors like family composition and responsibilities, professional development opportunities that will support school goals, and personal health and well-being issues.

> **Suggested Actions**: Set goals and timelines to achieve gender parity in leadership ranks in your school. Communicate about this publicly. Access resources and engage consultants to help make the case and to develop action steps. Follow through. Commit to, and develop policies and practices around, promoting and developing female leaders. Pay leaders, regardless of gender, the same for the same job. Be transparent about this. Tailor compensation packages to set leaders up for individual and school success.

Lesson 4: Womanize

While the word "womanize" has traditionally cast women into the victim role, we have an opportunity to transform the definition of "womanize" to one that empowers and includes all for the benefit of society as a whole. This is where the real rewards start.

If you've already created an environment where women feel safe, supported, valued, and included, chances are that *everyone* in the school community will feel that way. This is not a zero-sum game. Measures that benefit women do not need to be at the expense of men; indeed, they can lay the groundwork for a leadership culture—and therefore a school culture—that embraces feminine and masculine attributes and energies and allows them to flourish in a complementary, mutually reinforcing way.

What might *womanizing* mean in practice? It means reimagining the school landscape from a female perspective: a "her"spective. This can be broad, wide-ranging, all-encompassing. How might usage of space look different? What about the school calendar? Website? Admissions criteria? Food offerings? Pedagogy? Curricular content? Activity offerings? Learning assessment? Discipline? Communications? Recruitment? You get the gist.

There is no one right way to go about this (though there are plenty of wrong ones). I'd suggest taking a ground-up approach, including females from all stakeholder groups (leadership, faculty, students, staff, parents) and encouraging fresh, innovative thinking. You might want to involve a facilitator for the process. At some point, involve males. This should only be *after* females have provided their input.

The "her"spectives that come from this may surprise your school community. They may even surprise the females that provide their input. Chances are that some of the insights can be used right away, because they are so… obvious and accessible.

I'll leave this idea here for now to simmer. I'm keen to hear how it resonates and what it might lead to. I'll be here in my sidecar, ready to spread good ideas around the landscape. Let's see what grows!

Suggested Action: Go forth and womanize!

About Bridget McNamer

Bridget McNamer currently serves as Chief Navigation Officer for Sidecar Counsel, which aims to bring more women into leadership roles in international schools, enhance their leadership capacities once there, and cultivate an environment where women in these schools – and thereby all members of the school community – can thrive. Prior to creating Sidecar Counsel, she served as a senior associate with Search Associates and, in her earlier career, was an international philanthropy professional with more than 20 years' experience in advancing social change in the foundation, corporate responsibility and education sectors.

14

Learning, Friendship, and Transformation through Service

Equity and Cultural Responsiveness

Lisa Perskie

Arrayed in traditional Cameroon clothing with its brilliant patterns in orange-red, black, gold, white, and brown, three groups of fifth-grade students mount a stage overlooking an audience of 1,500 School of the Nations' community members and visitors. We are celebrating the annual Nations' Festival in which each grade level studies a country in the light of a global theme. Students engage in projects to explore the country's culture, arts, history, and even gastronomical customs. When possible, the students choose a country represented by a classmate to study and work with the embassy and a family from the country to learn more about the facets of its culture. On the day of the festival, the whole school becomes a museum for their projects, artifacts created by students, and foods from each nation represented.

Two hours are dedicated to onstage presentations. All the fifth-grade students are proudly wearing costumes native to Cameroon. However, the proudest of them all is Alex (name changed), a student from Cameroon who leads the group in a traditional dance to the beat of thunderous rhythms, as strong as elephants from Africa thundering through the crowds. Alex rules the stage and conquers the audience as he moves his whole body in syncopated rhythm with the music, his dark skin glistening and radiant, his smile a bolt of white, and his whole being transfigured with joy. He raises his hands as if connecting with heaven. The crowd goes wild over his uninhibited artistic expression, which has spread contagiously to the entire group that is stomping and dancing in time with Alex.

Before the festival, Alex was ashamed to tell people he was from Cameroon. He had learned Portuguese well enough to dissimulate as a Brazilian. Alex also had his share of discipline issues as he had an energy that sometimes seemed on par with nuclear fusion. However, his self-esteem was low, even though he might speak up loudly at times. We were worried and wanted him to know and feel that he did not have to be like anyone else to belong and relax into his skin more.

After this festival and the resounding standing ovation he received, followed by innumerable compliments about the dance, the dress, and his artistic leadership, Alex was glad to tell everyone he was from Cameroon from then on. He not only reconnected with his heritage and native land, but he was also more confident in his identity as a young man. This was an experience that he could always remember and relive. It was a turning point in his life.

Alex had provided a service to his peers, teaching them how to perform this dance. And his embassy helped students learn about a country they had never heard of before. As a result, they came to appreciate this new and, for most of them, very different culture. After the unit of study on Cameroon, our students gained broader and richer perspectives as world citizens.

Equity and Cultural Responsiveness

Hosting a Festival of Nations is one of many examples of how to foster intercultural understanding and promote equity. When we feel a sense of admiration and awe about another country and people so far away, so diverse, we begin to relate to them as members of one global family - the human race.

Equity and cultural responsiveness are pivotal themes in today's polarized world. Equity is an essential principle for achieving equality, fairness, and justice in any organization or social system. We need to understand the difference between equity and equality and act on it to ensure that our attempts to develop and maximize human potential are effective.

> "Equality means each individual or group of people is given the same resources or opportunities. Equity recognizes that each person has different circumstances and allocates the exact resources and opportunities needed to reach an equal outcome" (MPH@GW, the George Washington University online Master of Public Health program, 2020).

Most international schools' mission and values statements affirm the equality of rights and opportunities for all students. However, there is a blindness to equality without equity. Traditionally, it has meant uniformly applying the same standardized, one-size-fits-all educational delivery for students regardless of their backgrounds or special needs. We are still in the process of emerging from such an industrialized model of standardization in education: or, as Freire calls it, a banking education in which knowledge is deposited in students and withdrawn in tests (Freire, 2017). Consciously or unconsciously, by ignoring the reality of human diversity, we generate, as opposed to eliminating, inequalities and injustice over time.

Innumerable factors can impede or foster an individual's capacity to play on the same field and to enjoy the same benefits as others. These range from their overt physical disabilities to a wide range of physical, neurobiological, psychological, and cultural differences. There have been significant advances (laws, policy development, advocacy) in recognizing the needs of students with disabilities and clinically diagnosed disorders and providing services to them within regular school environments.

However, the most profound lessons that transform individuals like Alex and society go deeper into the "heart" of the matter of equity and cultural responsiveness. They venture past the checklists of politically correct dos and don'ts to know and understand other people's perspectives and realities. While most schools have wheelchair access everywhere on campus, not as many educate students on how to embrace their peers from all different backgrounds, ethnicities, and gender identities in school. We are still plagued by controversy about raising student awareness of the impacts and effects of inequities in society.

If our school's mission includes more than preparing students for the next level of education, we need to prepare them to see and engage with the world—a world in which they are actually a minority!

Scientific Underpinnings of Moral Imperative to Equity

We are still entering a new frontier of discovery about how diverse yet essentially connected we are as human beings. On the one hand, our species has been estimated to share 99.9 percent of our DNA (Chou, 2017). According to Bill Nye, the Science Guy, we all come from Africa and are made up of the same stardust. On the other hand, differences in background, gender identity, and cultural customs challenge us in embracing our shared humanity.

The oneness and unity of the human family do not mean sameness but rather wholeness and integration. A natural ecosystem is as healthy as the diversity of its flora and fauna. A human system should be enhanced and sustained, not threatened by diversity.

If we accept that we are members of one human species, then we will embrace the rights of all our family members. Equity, especially as it honors and protects human diversity, is at the basis of individual well-being and social justice.

Vital Principles for a Globally Interconnected World

In our school, like others of its kind, many of our students come from the top percent of the most socially and economically privileged families in the country. They are highly protected. The neighborhood where our school is located and in which most students live has been compared to a Disneyland of urban living. There is little in their daily existence to awaken awareness of the suffering caused by social inequities.

However, during the COVID-19 pandemic, curtains were pulled aside. We witnessed the intensity of the suffering of those living in the outlying, underserved, and disenfranchised neighborhoods with inadequate health care and technological infrastructure. One of our community members who lives in such an area lost both his father and sister in the same month, with his sister leaving two orphaned girls, while others in our community who had access to excellent medical services survived COVID.

In promoting students' social and cultural awareness, we take care to avoid the political minefield of polarized positions or sensationalizing the distress of much of humanity. We also look to steer clear of the extremes of militant activism, easy-to-digest slogans, and superficial acknowledgment of these social issues.

No simple formula or road map exists for fostering equity or overcoming cultural barriers. National and school laws can regulate services and opportunities for diverse people, but what people most need and want cannot be mandated. Celebrating an international day is only one way of evoking and symbolizing these values to the community. Equity and cultural responsiveness are best learned when people relate to people, share experiences, and serve together in meaningful projects and authentic situations requiring interaction and collaboration.

We thrive when we are connected, loved, and feel that we belong to a community. We grow when we serve others and contribute to society. The real lessons of equity and cultural responsiveness are learned when we leave the bubbles that seemingly protect us but separate us from others. We must open our hearts, change our comfort-driven habits, and reach out to those from different backgrounds and social realities.

Friendships are at the heart of sustainable practices of equity, inclusion, and cultural responsiveness. There is no substitute for caring and curious conversations, shared laughter, and consultations. Equity and justice are best developed by practicing the golden rule. When we befriend others and work on issues of common interest together, barriers melt away and new friendships blossom along with new solutions.

We need to practice the golden rule not only on the individual scale but on the social scale as well. To practice love, we must eliminate religious, racial, political, economic, and patriotic prejudices. Justice is often associated with force, but it is established by humble, truthful people who care about the welfare of others. If we look at societies that are more peaceful and prosperous than others, such as Norway, Switzerland, or Canada, we will see there is more justice and equity in their laws and culture. Peoples of all different backgrounds have access to the same opportunities and enjoy the same rights.

"We cannot segregate the human heart from the environment outside us and say that once one of these is reformed, everything will be improved. Man is organic with the world. His inner life molds the environment and is itself also deeply

155

affected by it. The one acts upon the other, and every abiding change in the life of man is the result of these mutual reactions." (Effendi, 1933,p.?)

At School of the Nations, we have embedded our mission and values to foster love, knowledge, and service to educate students as citizens of the world. We believe that moral development cannot happen in a vacuum. We need to interact with those from all different backgrounds and with the world. It is impossible to develop virtues and ethical qualities without putting them to the test in our actions. Our actions should be coherent with our words and what we profess to believe and value.

So How Do We Teach This in Our Schools?

Three decades in the field of international education have shown me that dramatic changes are occurring, if not in desk-filled classrooms then in the zeitgeist of the era—leading us to make a shift from me-centered, competitive, subject-driven education to we-inclusive, competency-based collaborative practices. The world is demanding of us to respond to its needs, from global issues like pandemics and rampant economic inequities to recognizing the full range of individual diversity.

Treating others equitably and respecting cultural diversity are moral imperatives of the age. However, they are behaviors that must be taught and cultivated consistently. We spend twelve years teaching students math, English, and other essential subjects for life in society. It requires a deep commitment on the part of the school governance and administration to embed the processes of inquiry, learning, and response needed to foster equity and to embrace cultural diversity in the school environment and culture. It is an ongoing, unending process!

We also need to know that the days of focusing only on the ABCs of schooling are gone. Universities and the marketplace now place premium value on the interpersonal and intrapersonal competencies of potential professionals (i.e., growth mindset, flexibility, collaboration, and communication skills).

As educators, we need to be at the forefront of understanding and relating to human diversity in its manifold forms! We must go beyond the delivery of services to building community within our schools and connecting to the wider world. Educators must build the capacity to understand and model the attitudes and practices we expect from our budding citizens of the world.

At our school, we have provided ongoing courses, workshops, and presentations on special education and social-emotional learning to sensitize teachers in fostering holistic and varied student learning experiences. However, the most powerful learning occurs through relationships and experiences extending beyond the classroom. A few examples of the ways we promote this development of equity, cultural understanding, and social responsibility follow.

Learning for Fun Project: This project is led by students. They work with the administration and teachers at a nearby school(s) to give English classes to students. Our students changed the project's name from English for Fun to Learning for Fun when they discovered they were learning as much or even more from the students and community they served. The English they were teaching was secondary to the quality of caring relationships they were developing.

Amazon Crossing: This marvelous project has been on hold for a few years. However, it has been characterized as one of the most impacting educational experiences ever experienced by those who have participated.

We established a partnership with the Amazon-based nongovernmental organization *Associação para o Avanço da*

Cidadania no Campo (AACC) located in Iranduba, Amazonia. The project involves sending students to participate in an ecological, intercultural learning experience. In groups of four to ten, students spend a week to ten days in the Amazon. Local youth from Amazon river communities serve as guides and teachers for our students to learn about survival in the forest - everything from climbing up a palm tree to preparing flour from *mandioca*. They also hear stories of great hardship and physical suffering, like planting crops for six months that may all be lost in a flood.

An English teacher accompanying a group wrote that the "lesson" our students learned about service is that they can make a difference in other peoples' lives by their presence and mutual relationships. They found that service need not be the act of one person or group giving another "something." In fact, in the act of giving things, you can take on a superior stance as if you are the better, bigger person helping the other. The recipient is not empowered. Service can also come in the form of sharing and learning mutually in a friendly relationship. We can best help people by showing them their capacities and capabilities to solve problems.

UNAtions Project: In 2018, we began an educational extension project called UNAtions, which stands for "Unite" and "Nations" (our school name). We wanted UNAtions to be a project developed by educators for educators to share their knowledge, experiences, and methods to promote children's learning, development, and ability to contribute to serving and improving society. Our goal was to work with a few schools and those interested in developing long-term relationships. All would take a mutually active role in developing and strengthening educational environments and practices to benefit children.

This project has transformed the participants and one school in the Amazon, in particular, as a school system. The *Escola do Futuro* in Manaus was able to retain almost all its students during the

COVID-19 pandemic in large part through the training we provided on methods of distance learning and online teaching.

Interdisciplinary Projects: You can learn any subject through the lens of questions and issues in today's world. We promote interdisciplinary projects that center on or are aligned with one of the UN Global Goals for sustainable development. Students research the issues and compare what other countries are doing with their own country's initiatives.

The academic lens to teaching equity we offer should be based on research, the use of primary resources, interviews, and visits to communities.

Model United Nations Club: The simulations teach students how the United Nations works.

Daily homeroom, advisory classes, and assemblies that center on both social-emotional and "social" themes are nonacademic but focused learning forums for students to discuss issues, understand themselves better, and gain capacities to handle the complex issues facing them in today's tumultuous world.

Empathy is a particularly important capacity for our students, whose privileged lives can sometimes narrow their worldview and lead to self-centered attitudes.

"Empathy is an important component of social and emotional learning and challenging academic skill. To empathize requires understanding others in their context, overcoming personal biases, asking important questions, and seeking new learning." (Priddy, 2018, p. 102).

Absorb Kindness: A service initiative called Absorb Kindness was launched by three Nations students, supported by their moral education teachers, to provide female prisoners with hygiene products. Prison administrators shared that often there were not enough personal hygiene products for all. Over half the women, therefore, do not receive sanitary pads. Students heard about this issue and researched social media networks to find testimonials of these women and learn more about their situation and how they might help.

Later, our Nations Girl Up group helped a district deputy draft the law that calls for free distribution of sanitary napkins in Basic Health Units (UBS) for women who are at risk and in public schools.

The world is crying for justice, wisdom, and love. Our schools have the opportunity to go beyond teaching subjects to educating students for their roles as citizens and ethical leaders. Students can be informed of social issues and involved in so many constructive ways, primarily through service in other neighborhoods to develop ongoing relationships. At our school, we encourage students' individual personal growth to be aligned with the development of their moral values and social commitments.

Students must venture out of the bastions of knowledge we call schools and the guarded enclaves we call homes - through Zoom or in person, opening windows of investigation and understanding into the world around them. When students embrace the equal value of others different from them, they will discover the latent power in equity - the power of unity in diversity. Minds and hearts will connect to generate creative possibilities of all kinds. In the end, we are beautifully diverse, *and* we are one!

Chou, V. (2017, April 17). *How science and genetics are reshaping the race debate of the 21st century*. Retrieved from Harvard University Graduate School of Arts and Sciences: https://sitn.hms.harvard.edu/flash/2017/science-genetics-reshaping-race-debate-21st-century/

Effendi, S. (1933, February 17). Letter written on behalf of Shoghi Effendi. *Compilation on Social and Economic Development*, p. 4.

Freire, P. (2017). *Pedagogy of the oppressed*. Penguin Classics.

MPH@GW, the George Washington University online Master of Public Health program. (2020, November 5). *Equity vs. equality: What's the difference?* Retrieved December 7, 2021, from GW Online Public Health: https://onlinepublichealth.gwu.edu/resources/equity-vs-equality/

Priddy, N. (2018, December). Empathy is academic: Lessons from lotus slippers. *Education Update*, 60(12).

About Lisa Perskie

Lisa Perskie Rodriguez is serving her eighteenth year as Executive Director of School of the Nations, a Bahá'í-inspired, N-12, bilingual, international school in Brasilia, Brazil. Previously, she was Middle School Principal at the American School of Guatemala and Director of Colegio Panamericano in Bucaramanga, Colombia, S.A. Her background includes experience as an Elementary and Pre-School Principal at Colegio Panamericano in Bucaramanga, Colombia, and elementary teacher at Colegio Albania, Colombia. She has thirty years of experience in international education.

Ms. Perskie holds a Master's Degree in Educational Administration from Plymouth State College, New Hampshire, a Specialization in Teaching English as a Foreign Language in Elementary School from the Universidad Industrial de Santander, Bucaramanga, Colombia, S.A., and a BA Degree from Hamilton College in Art History. She studied in a one-year Art History program through Syracuse University in Italy during college. After earning her BA, she pursued two years of postgraduate studies in Art History at Indiana University with a concentration in pre-renaissance art. She has a technical degree in commercial photography and is fluent in English, Spanish, and Portuguese. She has served seven times on Cognia (formerly AdvancEd) accreditation teams in several countries. She has four grandchildren and recently completed her first young adult novel.

15

Getting Down to Business: An Institutional Approach to Organizational Management for School Leaders

Operations and Resource Management

Dr. Ruth Allen

Like many heads of school, I had little to no formal training in business management when I first assumed the role. As a result, during financial presentations to the board, my brain seemed to process the information one step behind everyone else's. By the time I had made sense of the numbers on the screen and the jargon being thrown around the room (in Spanish), the conversation had moved on. In some cases, decisions had been made before I even knew they were on the table. Fairly soon I found myself sliding into a state of resignation. No one else seemed particularly perturbed by the fact that I wasn't really keeping up, so I began to feel that maybe my role in the leadership of the school was, after all, purely academic, limited to reporting on progress in terms of pedagogy and student performance. I would leave the "business" to others.

However, after describing the situation to a more experienced head of school, I was cautioned to take care. "Just be aware," I was told, "whoever is in control of the budget is really in control of the school." Indeed, the dangers of deferring key school decisions to individuals whose primary focus is financial

(Macdonald, 2008) soon became apparent at one memorable meeting. Having been tasked with finding some efficiencies in the budget, the business manager presented a project for reducing the length of teacher contracts. The argument was, "We don't pay truck drivers when they are not driving the trucks, so why should we pay teachers when they are not teaching the students?" Suddenly, I found a voice. Thankfully, the board president was fully aware of the professional implications of a teacher's work and understood that the scope of that work went well beyond the classroom walls. The project was not approved. However, as I reflected on the situation, my relief was tempered by a burgeoning sense of unease. I had been blindsided by this proposal. My opinion had been overlooked. Had I not been consulted because the business manager felt I lacked authority regarding business issues? Was the lack of consultation a deliberate attempt to cancel out my voice? It seemed that my passive approach to organizational affairs had resulted in the business manager becoming more active, assuming a position of greater influence and effectively filling the void in leadership. While some of these thoughts were undoubtedly the result of my own insecurities rather than any deliberate attempt to sabotage my position, it was clear that the burgeoning sense of unease was undermining my trust in the team. Something had to change. My approach to the management of school business matters had to become more strategic.

My first challenge was simply to overcome a sense of inadequacy. I looked for external support and received professional development through which I learned how to read financial statements and understand the implications of financial indicators. However, it was also unrealistic to think that I would become an expert in accounting or develop skills that might match those of the business manager. The real priority was to find ways in which I could create a "closer, symbiotic relationship" (Starr, 2014, p. 38) between the academic team and that of the business office. The challenge was to find ways in which the educators could feel comfortable with finance being foregrounded and where those in the business office could feel the professional requirements of their role were recognized and respected.

Caffyn (2018) argues that most international schools are private businesses and, as such, are placed on an uneasy borderland between economic and learning goals. He argues that these borderland zones are "conduits of power and energy" (p. 502), channeling differences of attitudes, opinions, and values and are fraught with tension and conflict. However, while tensions and conflict will undoubtedly exist, it is also important to recognize that the business and academic aspects of a school are inexorably linked. On the one hand, all decisions related to learning, such as the implementation of a particular pedagogical model or the organization and structure of the schedule, have a financial consequence. On the other, all financial decisions, such as those related to the salary structure or even the management of transport and cafeteria, have an impact on learning. Even in nonprofit schools, economic factors are vital to ensuring survival in an increasingly uncertain and precarious global context. Finding the right balance between financial and learning goals would therefore seem to be critical, and critical to this balance would seem to be the relationship between the head of school and the business manager.

In many international schools, the business manager is the only member of the leadership team who is not an educator. The business manager is also likely to be a host country national with a high level of cultural competency in the local context. They may have well-established relationships within the school community and even with members of the board, being cognizant of the dynamics between board members and possible reactions to change. For the head of school, establishing and maintaining trust with the business manager is, therefore, key to the operations of the school, the organizational climate, and the successful management of change. Unfortunately, in the world of international schools, stories of conflict and tensions between heads of school and their colleagues in the business office abound. In one school, I saw how differences of opinions and values damaged the relationship between the head of school and business manager to the point at which they could no longer speak to one another. Instead, they sent messages through third parties even when they were in the same room. This was not only unhealthy for the organization but also for the individuals involved. Neither remained at the school for very long. I have also seen how tempting it can be for heads of school (myself included) to distance themselves from "business" decisions, allowing blame to be apportioned to a business office which then runs the risk of being seen as an unfeeling, faceless bureaucracy. This is neither fair nor sustainable for those involved. So, what is necessary for a successful relationship between the business office and the head of the school? How might trust be established? What systems and structures could be implemented to maintain that trust over time? While trust can certainly be strengthened at a personal level, I suggest that taking a strategic perspective by approaching the issue through a process of "institutionalization" can help to create more sustainable structures and mitigate the risks of conflict in the long term, regardless of the individual relationships involved.

According to Scott (2014), institutionalization processes involve the establishment of three "pillars" that form the "central building blocks" (p. 57) of the organization, providing structure and stability. These pillars are defined as the regulative pillar, the normative pillar, and the cultural-cognitive pillar. (See Figure 1.) The regulative pillar refers to the establishment of rules and regulations. It is what most of us think of when we seek to establish policies and procedures that will allow for smooth operations and avoid a conflict of interest between individuals within an organization. The normative pillar refers to the establishment of institutional values and the implementation of

166

standards of professional behavior. It provides guidance for decisions and organizational behaviors that go beyond expectations of regulatory compliance. The cultural-cognitive pillar refers to the development of shared beliefs and understandings. Through shared cultural-cognitive understandings, individuals within an organization can make sense of a situation and are able to act with confidence and conviction, certain in the knowledge that they can count on the support and understanding of their colleagues. Identifying the aspects of business operations that fall into these categories can facilitate the implementation of actions needed to strengthen institutional effectiveness and ensure harmony between those responsible for the business and academic goals of a school.

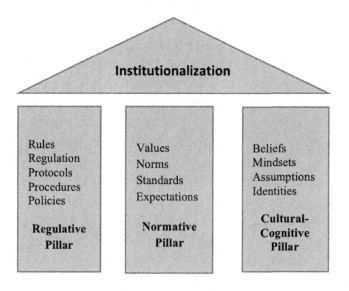

Figure 1. The Pillars of Institutionalization
Source: Based on Scott 2003, 2014.

In terms of the regulative pillar, having clear rules and regulations for financial management is often a legal requirement for many schools. It might, therefore, be considered an area unlikely to generate conflict and tension. However, it is important not to assume that all members of staff, particularly those who do not have a background in the business world, are familiar with such requirements. Indeed, heads of school may find themselves caught between a business office that requires strict processes and procedures for resource acquisition and academic staff who see those processes and procedures as bureaucratic obstacles, standing in the way of what they need to do a good job in the classroom. This problem is often exacerbated by the fact that budgets need to be established well in advance of a new academic year, a fact that can be frustrating for academic staff, potentially contradicting the message that they should adapt and adjust their practices to incorporate the needs of students. For example, an analysis of student performance results based on the Advanced Placement exams or the International Baccalaureate Diploma Program may indicate a need for more targeted professional development or more staffing in student support. However, as these results are not received until long after most budgets have been approved, adjustments to the established budget may be difficult, or even impossible, to make within a time scale that seems acceptable to teachers.

Another important aspect of the regulative pillar is that any established rules and regulations must be aligned with the primary task of an organization (Bunnell et al., 2017). In the case of successful business management in schools, this means ensuring all processes and procedures are designed to support the primary task of teaching and learning. In line with this, many accreditation agencies require that schools demonstrate their budgeting procedures are aligned with the mission and purpose of the organization, encouraging participative budget preparation processes that accommodate teacher and student needs. However, while collaborative budget preparation may be a common practice, the processes, and procedures necessary for effective budget execution are often overlooked. To consolidate processes in this area we might ask, for example "How far is the budget decentralized to allow for academic staff a level of control over the financial resources they have been assigned?"; "What processes and procedures are in place to allow for flexibility if adjustments are required?"; and "Who authorizes those adjustments and based on what criteria?" Coming to agreement on how these issues will be addressed can potentially avoid situations where academic staff circumvent processes they find frustrating and result in errors that create administrative issues.

While establishing clear rules and regulations can prevent people from making mistakes in organizational management, it is also important to identify what steps will be taken when those errors inevitably occur (we are human after all). Administrative errors can be costly to the school (the principal who miscalculates staffing needs and hires an additional person) or minimal to the school but costly to staff (the staff member who hands in a receipt without the required information and then has expenses deducted from the payroll). Brushing mistakes under the carpet with a shrug and a reference to "academics" lacking in administrative expertise will not only undermine the established rules and regulations but also the credibility of business procedures themselves. At the same time, leaping into disciplinary procedures when an error may be the result of an honest mistake can have detrimental consequences for all concerned. Identifying in anticipation how these situations will be dealt with can prevent a simple situation from spiraling out of control.

Another practice that can potentially be damaging to the relationship between the business office and the head of school is when those at the higher levels of authority step outside established policies and procedures simply assuming they have the autonomy to do so. A head of school who negotiates an individual salary package with a teaching candidate to secure their number one choice or a business manager who makes investments in classroom technology without considering instructional needs are both examples of people in power stepping outside established policies and procedures. Being clear about the levels of autonomy and flexibility each individual might be allocated is vital, and communication is key. We may be acting within our established scope of authority, but we should always ask ourselves, "Just because I can do this, is it right that I do so?" Taking time to review a decision with colleagues, even when our level of authority does not require that we do so, may not only be courteous but may also help to avoid potential errors of judgment. Indeed, relying on one another as "critical friends" is a key part of the relationship between the business manager and head of school.

Having clarity in terms of who might have the final word on business-related decisions is also vital. While it is often assumed that the "buck" stops with the head of school, this is often not the case. Some schools (particularly those in the for-profit sector) may have the figure of a CEO or an external office that manages finance at a higher level. Indeed, the policies and procedures of most schools (whether for-profit or not) are likely to stipulate that the board must approve decisions that have major financial implications. In these circumstances, ensuring agreement between the business manager and the head of school before entering the boardroom is critical. Using the board as judge and jury on whether one is right and the other wrong is likely to end in "divorce" or disaster.

Actions within the normative pillar of institutionalization seek to strengthen the norms and values of an organization, establishing standards and expectations for professional behavior. Critical to this area is perceived alignment between the values espoused by the organization and the practices it employs (Jondle et al., 2013). When the business practices in a school are not aligned with declared values, the organization's reputation may be put at risk and perceptions of its legitimacy questioned. For example, many international schools declare trust and transparency as core values, but few have salary and benefit structures that are transparent and open for public review. Many espouse equity but have yet to resolve issues of differences in remuneration for local and expatriate staff. Full transparency and equity in these areas may be a long-term goal for many international schools but are undoubtedly difficult to achieve, particularly while schools face a volatile global financial context. Nonetheless, various strategies can be implemented to mitigate the risks of perceived organizational hypocrisy (Brunsson, 1986). For example, rather than leaving the salary to be structured in isolation by the business office, Littleford (2020) advocates using a collaborative process that includes the business office, academic staff, and board members to establish a "philosophy of compensation" that ensures systems of remuneration reflect the mission and values of the institution. Having a cross-disciplinary group allows for the identification of factors that might be taken into consideration beyond traditional qualifications and experience. These factors might include "innovation in teaching," "mentoring of fellow teachers," and simply "going the extra mile" (p. 1). Implementing a collaborative process of this type increases confidence in the system and creates a shared understanding of the *how* and *why* of the salary structure, establishing clarity of purpose among all members of staff.

Students are also likely to be sensitive to organizational hypocrisy. For example, claims within a school's mission to form global citizens who care about the environment and are concerned about sustainability can quickly be undermined when single-use plastics are used in the cafeteria or green spaces devoured to develop a parking lot for staff. Involving students in discussions with the business office and including their voices in decision-making around this type of issue can be a great learning experience for all concerned and can ensure that business decisions are more closely aligned with strategic goals.

Another area in which it is important to establish standards and norms is risk management, particularly as related to student safety. Safety and security are often within the remit of the business office; however, a desire to minimize risk can sometimes clash with pedagogical expectations and practices. For example, after a workshop on the management of risk, one business manager decided to remove all the play equipment from the Early Years play area, citing the risk of possible accidents. A line of small, very grumpy faces at the door of the business office soon overturned that decision but also consolidated teachers' perceptions of the business manager as being detached from the reality of schooling. Another business manager consistently opposed the organization of school trips, arguing that the risks were too great and the benefits too small to justify such activities. Teachers became frustrated that their initiatives were not supported and criticized the business office for limiting their potential to offer valuable opportunities for experiential learning. Simply overriding the concerns of the business manager ran the risk of undermining their credibility with staff and, in this case, alternative strategies needed to be employed. First, the school implemented a system for the evaluation of risk that included identifying levels of tolerance toward risk and actions for its mitigation. Second, the business manager was encouraged to join students on a school trip. After witnessing the impact of outdoor education firsthand, the previously skeptical individual was converted. It became clear that involving business staff in academic activities could be transformative and equally as valuable as involving academic staff and/or students in business affairs.

The third pillar of institutionalization, the cultural-cognitive pillar, is rarely addressed in relation to the business of schools but can be central to establishing shared understandings that may strengthen the organization. Questions that might be asked include, "What are our beliefs about how organizations work?"; "What is our approach to organizational management?"; and "How does our organizational structure reflect our beliefs about power and authority?" Fidan and Balci (2018) argue that schools are highly complex social organizations that are characterized by uncertainty and unpredictability. As such, they require an organic approach to organizational management that allows for natural growth and development rather than a strictly mechanical approach based upon command and control. This may be unfamiliar to staff in the business office who may be accustomed to more predictable environments and a more classical, authoritative management style. Discussing the differences between these management approaches and agreeing upon which should be employed and under what circumstances is likely to set a solid foundation for successful teamwork.

A shared understanding of the concept of leadership structures is also critical. Many traditional corporations and businesses are built upon the traditional pyramid design, having a small number of leaders at the top, followed by middle managers, and then a wide range of basic employees on the bottom line. However, this type of structure would once again seem to be inappropriate for schools. Flipping, or inverting the pyramid and ensuring that the leaders (including those in the business office) are seen to be supporting the front-line teachers in the work they do, will lead to a much more mission-based approach that respects the professional status of educators and ensures a focus on student learning.

Finally, involving the business manager and other staff from the business office in key conversations related to teaching and learning is vital. Shared understandings of the basic concepts of teaching and learning, such as how a particular pedagogical model might relate to the school's vision and purpose, will allow for greater levels of support from the business office and permit alternative perspectives to be incorporated into the school's plans.

Despite the knowledge and experience gained since those early days as a head of school, I admit that there are still moments during discussions about finance that my brain seems to lag behind those of the experts in the room. However, I have learned that as a head of school I cannot be passive in financial matters, and that while it may seem "counter-intuitive" (Macdonald, 2008, p. 52) for an educational leader to take a business perspective, it is only by "getting down to business" that we can truly have an impact on our school's vision and purpose. I have also learned that any lack of fiduciary skills on my part does not need to represent a potential loss of control. Indeed, the development of a high level of personal and professional trust with the business manager renders the concept of "control" redundant. When disagreements arise (as they inevitably do), the institutional approach means that we can take a solution-oriented perspective rather than allowing conflicts and tensions to arise. Using the analytical structure provided by the three pillars of institutionalization we can ask these questions:

- "Do we need to review related rules and regulations?"
- "Is our discomfort the result of a lack of alignment with established professional expectations, or mission-oriented goals and values?"
- "Is it necessary to take time out to identify any differences in beliefs and assumptions that may be presenting an obstacle to our agreement?"

This strategic perspective is successful as it removes the "personal," consolidates the "professional," and facilitates an effective approach to organizational management that enriches the educational experience for all.

Brunsson, N. (1986). Organizing for inconsistencies: On organizational conflict, depression and hypocrisy as substitutes for action. *Scandinavian Journal of Management Studies*, 2(3), 165–185.

Bunnell, T., Fertig, M. & James, C. (2017) Establishing the legitimacy of a school's claim to be "International": The provision of an international curriculum as the institutional primary task. Educational Review 69.3: 303-17.

Caffyn, R. (2018). "The shadows are many . . ." Vampirism in international school leadership: Problems and potential in cultural, political, and psycho-social borderlands. *Peabody Journal of Education*, 93(5), 500–517.

Fidan, T., & Balci, A. (2018). School administrators as legitimation agents: Linking perceived organizational legitimacy and legitimation strategies. *Educational Sciences: Theory & Practice*, 18(2), 253–277.

Jondle, D., Maines, T. D., Burke, M. R., & Young, P. (2013). Modern risk management through the lens of the ethical organizational culture. *Risk Management*, 15(1), 32–49.

Littleford, J. (2020, July 1). Why we will have failed them: How to regain faculty trust. https://www.jlittleford.com/why-we-will-have-failed-them-how-to-regain-faculty-trust/

Macdonald, J. (2008). A cure for insomnia. *Journal of Research in International Education*, 7(1), 37–54.

Scott, W. R. (2003). Institutional carriers reviewing modes of transporting ideas over time and space and considering their consequences. *Industrial and Corporate Change*, 12(4), 879–894.

Scott, W. R. (2014). *Institutions and organizations: Ideas, interests, and identities* (4th ed.). Sage.

Starr, K. (2014). The role of business officials in school leadership. *School Business Affairs*. https://www.academia.edu/27197075/The_role_of_business_officials_in_school_leadership

About Dr. Ruth Allen

Dr. Allen has over 30 years of experience as an educator in both the UK and Colombia. After various roles including HS teacher, Curriculum Coordinator and HS Principal, Dr. Allen has now served as a Head of School for 16 years. She is currently Superintendent at The Columbus School, Medellin, Colombia.

Dr. Allen holds an MA in Language Studies from the University of Lancaster, and an MSc in Multidisciplinary studies from SUNY, Buffalo. She earned her doctorate from the University of Bath, where she focused on educational leadership, administration, and the concept of establishing institutional legitimacy in international schools. She was awarded the Jeff Thompson Prize for her thesis.

Dr Allen has served as a Cognia lead evaluator on accreditation reviews for several years and was previously chair of the AdvancED Latin American Council.

16

About the Authors

Catarina Song Chen

Lindsay Prendergast

Dr. Wallace Ting

About the Author

Catarina Song Chen

Catarina Song Chen has been working in the world of education for a quarter of a century in various roles such as classroom teacher, adjunct professor, and advisory board member. She is currently working as the Head of School at EABH (Escola Americana de Belo Horizonte) for the past 13 years.

Catarina holds a Bachelor of Arts in Philosophy from UCLA (University of California at Los Angeles), a Master's degree in Educational Leadership from Pepperdine University, and was awarded the Klingenstein fellowship from Columbia University.

Her entrepreneurial spirit and personal philosophy that learning must be fun have consequently led her to earn the National Distinguished Principal Award from NAESP (National Association of Elementary School Principals). Catarina has also been awarded a Certificate of Appreciation Award by the Undersecretary of Management from the U.S. Department of State and the International Education Leadership Award from AMISA (American International Schools in the Americas).

Outside of EABH, Catarina has served as Vice President of the Board of Trustees for AMISA, President of the Association of American Schools in Brazil, and is currently a board member for AAIE (Association for the Advancement of International Education), AISH (Academy for International School Heads), and SchoolRubric. Catarina has also served as an accrediting member for Cognia and Middle States Association. Her favorite pastimes include engaging as a course facilitator. She has taught education classes for UCLA and USC (University of Southern California), both located in Southern California. Catarina has also offered courses for AMISA and AISH for Aspiring School Heads. Her first publication includes an excerpt for Drs. Robyn Hansen and Frank Davidson's book from Routledge publishing company, *Principal's Desk Reference*, based on the National Policy Board for Educational Administration.

Born in Seoul, South Korea, raised in Asuncion, Paraguay and in Los Angeles, USA, she now resides in Belo Horizonte, Brazil with her husband Tim and two children Lucas and Tatiana.

About the Author

Lindsay Prendergast

Lindsay Prendergast, M.Ed., has served schools and districts across the globe for nearly two decades as a consultant, Principal, Counselor, and teacher. She currently supports leaders in one of the largest districts in the US as an embedded leadership coach for NWEA. Lindsay is also a Framework Specialist for The Danielson Group, an ASCD Emerging Leader, and a fellow with the Association for the Advancement of International Education (AAIE). Prior to NWEA, Lindsay served as a Principal of an international school in the Dominican Republic. She holds a Bachelor's degree from Wofford College and a Master's degree in Education Administration from Colorado Western University.

Lindsay is the Producer of SchoolRubric's flagship live education-focused show which brings about idea-exchange around the most important topics in our field with leading voices such as Dr. Yong Zhao, Homa Tavangar, Ewan McIntosh, and more. She regularly publishes and presents on leadership development and other topics for organizations including ASCD, AMLE, Learning Forward, EARCOS, Cognia and others.

Lindsay currently splits her time between Moab, Utah, Savannah, Georgia and Las Vegas, Nevada with her husband, Pete, and their spotted dog, Dingo.

About the Author

Dr. Wallace Ting

Dr. Wallace Ting is the co-founder of SchoolRubric, a 501c(3) non-profit organization that publishes articles, magazines, podcasts, courses, books, and other educational content from educators across the world. Dr. Ting graduated with a degree in Electrical Engineering from the University of Texas at Austin and earned two Master's degrees in Mathematics Education and Educational Administration and Leadership. His doctorate degree was awarded by the University of Southern California (USC) in Los Angeles, where he researched factors that impact international school director turnover and retention.

Prior to Dr. Ting's current role at SchoolRubric, he spent seven years in public education as a secondary mathematics teacher in Texas and New York City, along with 10 years overseas as a teacher, principal, deputy head, and superintendent in international schools in Colombia, Guatemala, and Nigeria. He has also worked at the university level teaching courses, leading school certification teams, and conducting research and assessment activities.

Dr. Ting currently lives and resides in Orlando, Florida with his son, Phillip. He dedicates this book to his late father, Sam Ting, who always believed in the empowerment of education and the good in others.

17

About SchoolRubric

Connecting the Dots to Make the World a Smaller Place

SchoolRubric was founded in 2019 by a group of international educators returning to the United States after spending over a decade living and working in international schools with a desire to remain connected with the friends and colleagues they had developed across the world.

Today, SchoolRubric remains true to its original vision to connect educators across the world through storytelling, sharing of best practices, and curation of high-quality educational content. We strongly believe in asking big questions across a global context that can be adapted and applied in individualized settings, and that there is more that unites the world of education than divides us.

Our community continues to grow, and we currently publish blogs, magazines, podcasts, courses, webinars, school spotlights, and more in both English and Spanish. We invite you to visit us at schoolrubric.org (English) or schoolrubric.es (Spanish) to learn more.

Printed in Great Britain
by Amazon

37053934R00109